OPEN
Costa Rica

by Charlie Morris

Open Road Travel Guides – designed for the
amount of time you *really* have for your trip!

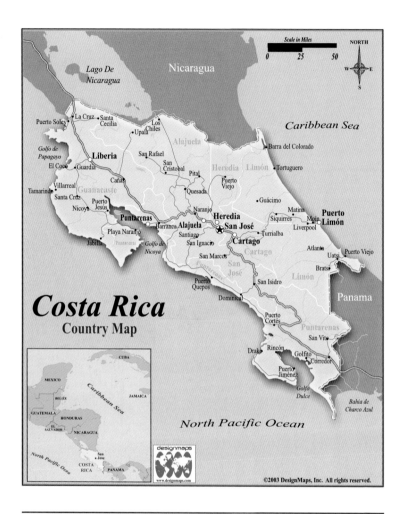

Costa Rica
Country Map

Text Copyright © 2006 by Charlie Morris
- All Rights Reserved -
ISBN 1-59360-068-2
Library of Congress Control No. 2006929101

Maps by designmaps.com. Photos © ShutterStock.com except on pages 1
(bottom center), 18, 21, 22, 24, 26, 29, 31, 8, 43, 49, 50, 55, 56, 59, 84, 90, 91, 98, 99,
101, 107, 175, 180, 188, 192 courtesy of Bruce Morris (brucemorris.com) and
pages 1 (bottom right), 73 78, 94, 185 courtesy of Laura Stein.

CONTENTS

Your Passport to the **Perfect Trip!**

Maps

1. INTRODUCTION

Costa Rica is a **tropical paradise** with the comforts of civilization. All the wonderful attractions of the tropics are here: sun-soaked beaches, azure seas, laughing monkeys, brightly-colored flowers and birds, the magical sound of palm fronds rustling in a gentle breeze. Many of the hassles that plague other tropical destinations are absent, or at least much less severe: Costa Rica is far less poor than her neighbors, and that means less crime and fewer aggressive hustlers. Tourist facilities are well developed: you'll have no problems getting around the country by small plane or rented car, finding excellent lodgings with all the modern amenities, and enjoying delightful local or international cuisine.

Costa Rica welcomes a huge number of visitors every year, most of whom come to experience her vast treasury of natural wonders. The rain forests hold **a stunning array of flora and fauna** (to give just one example, Costa Rica has more species of birds than the entire continent of North America), from playful monkeys to gaudy scarlet macaws to elusive wild cats. The seas teem with tropical fish. The volcanoes show nature at her most spectacular. There's a vast variety of landscapes, from sparkling beaches to coastal swampland to high mountains carpeted with lush greenery.

But the greatest asset of this peaceful and serene country is **her people**. The natives, called "Ticos," are some of the friendliest folks you'll meet anywhere. They've built a relatively prosperous nation, which has had a stable democracy for longer than any other Latin American country, and which has avoided the civil wars that have plagued her neighbors. Costa Rica has the best and most peaceful government of any country south of Canada.

The **activities are endless**. Fishing is spectacular, from tarpon and snook on the Caribbean coast to billfish in the Pacific. Surfing conditions are some of the best in the world, and kiteboarders find constant breezes on Lake Arenal. The rivers offer everything from breathless whitewater rafting to peaceful wildlife-observation trips through the jungle. The **beautiful mountain landscapes** are perfect for hiking, horseback riding and mountain biking.

Of course, many travelers also enjoy more sedate pursuits, such as sipping a cool drink while basking on a beautiful beach, and the opportunities for doing that in Costa Rica are second to none.

2. OVERVIEW

Costa Rica has a huge variety of astonishing scenery and climates for such a small country. You can visit the volcanoes and cloud forests of the central highlands, then explore the pristine beaches of the Pacific, all on the same trip. There are all kinds of fun activities for all interests and all levels of strenuousness. If you want to get deep in the jungle and be an ecotourist, or if your tastes run to action sports such as surfing, kiteboarding, diving, fishing or whitewater rafting, you can find the trip of a lifetime here. Along the way, you'll find pleasant and comfortable accommodations, sophisticated cuisine, exotic nightlife and a bit of shopping.

San José
Although there are a few things of interest in the capital city of **San José**, the best things for visitors to Costa Rica are found outside the cities. Even though it lacks the worst sort of third-world slums and poverty, San José is basically an unattractive city with few tourist diversions. Since most flights from North America arrive in San José in the afternoon, usually too late to catch a flight or drive to more salubrious areas of the country, most visitors find themselves spending at least one night in town.

Tip: Although there are some good hotels in town, more peaceful and pleasant hotels and lodges can be found in the suburbs and further out, some convenient to the airport.

The Central Valley

The **Central Valley** is a green patchwork of coffee plantations, tropical forests and well-ordered farms, dotted with small cities. It's here that most of the population, and almost all of the industry, is concentrated. There are numerous things of interest for tourists within the Central Valley, including volcanoes, waterfalls, whitewater rafting, coffee plantations, rain forest tours, butterfly farms and other wildlife-viewing opportunities.

North Caribbean Coast

The northeast of the country is a wild and roadless region of lowland marshes and jungles. Here you'll find some of the world's finest and most colorful fishing camps. Anglers battle it out with enormous tarpon and snook. Lovers of wildlife can take a jungle cruise through **Tortuguero National Park** or **Barra del Colorado National Wildlife Refuge**. The wild and deserted beaches of the region are important nesting sites for four different species of sea turtles.

South Caribbean Coast

South of the city of Limón, you'll find some of the most spectacular beaches in the country, and young people enjoying the Jamaican-flavored lifestyle. The area around **Cahuita** and **Puerto Viejo** offers excellent surfing, as well as beautiful coral reefs for diving and snorkeling. Remote wildlife reserves attract serious ecotourists.

North Central Region

The northern interior of Costa Rica includes some of her most famous sights. **Arenal** is one of the world's most active volcanoes. The nearby lake is one of the world's premier windsurfing and kiteboarding locales. **Monteverde Cloud Forest Preserve** is one of the country's most popular national parks. While this region is well trodden by tourist hordes, it's not hard to escape the crowds and get off the beaten path.

North Pacific Coast

The remote beaches of the **Nicoya Peninsula** are famous for both luxury resorts and down-to-earth hangouts for surfers and aging hippies. The climate is drier than other parts of the country, but there are lots of lush tropical forests with wildlife and birds aplenty. Two highlights are **Santa Rosa National Park** at the northwest corner of the country, and **Cabo Blanco Reserve** at the tip of the peninsula.

Central Pacific Coast

The central Pacific region is convenient to San José, and attracts lots of visitors to the young beach town of **Jacó** and the more upscale beach/tropical forest area of **Manuel Antonio**. Tourists flock to the coast to surf, party, lounge around the pool with umbrella drinks, watch whales or view wildlife on hikes and jungle cruises. Honeymooners come to posh hotels that rival those of Hawaii. **Los Sueños Marina** and **Quepos** are known for some of the best fishing in the world for sailfish, marlin and dorado.

South Pacific Coast

The remote and relatively unspoiled **Osa Peninsula** is the best place in the country to view wildlife and primary rain forest. Jungle lodges accessible only by boat, plane or on foot cater to both luxury and backpacking travelers. Monkeys go about their business in the trees, as toucans and scarlet macaws fly about for all to see. Here you'll also find fantastic fishing and secret, spectacular surfing spots.

The Switzerland of Central America

This nickname was coined because of Costa Rica's relative affluence and lack of political violence, but it could also refer to the vast variety of terrain in such a small area (or, perhaps, the number of Swiss expatriates living in the country).

In a region that includes some of the Western Hemisphere's poorest nations, Costa Rica's economy, literacy rate and life expectancy compare favorably with those of so-called "first-world" countries. Ticos enjoy state-funded medical insurance and a social security plan.

Although neighboring Nicaragua, El Salvador and Guatemala endured bloody civil wars in the late 20th Century, Costa Rica abolished its army in 1948. President Óscar Arias won the Nobel

Peace Prize in 1987 for his help in ending the seemingly eternal civil unrest in the region.

Why is Costa Rica such a success story? Everyone has a pet theory, but in the final analysis, there seems to be no secret other than hard work and clean living or, as the Ticos would say, *pura vida*.

Wildlife
Partly thanks to its affluence and political stability, Costa Rica has done an excellent job of protecting its natural beauty and wildlife. National parks and nature reserves cover more than a quarter of the land area. This small country has a huge variety of different climates and ecosystems, and the parks have been planned to preserve at least a sample of each one. Although most wildlife is elusive, visitors can expect to see parrots, crocodiles, agoutis, coatis, monkeys, sloths, Jesus Christ lizards, and iguanas. The lucky may see anteaters, pacas, ocelots, dolphins or whales.

Bird Watching
With over 870 (and counting) bird species available for viewing, it is impossible for even the most hard-core birder to visit Costa Rica without adding significantly to their life list. Multicolored scarlet macaws and toucans, along with a wide assortment of Little Brown Birds (LBBs), flit through the forest, and vast flocks of shorebirds patrol the coasts. If the birding gods smile on you, you may even see a quetzal, trogon, or ferruginous pygmy owl. Many lodges and tour companies cater specifically to birders.

Canopy Tours
Whether it is by zip line, elevated walkway or other means, tours of the rain forest canopy are all the rage. Most wildlife will be seen

further away from areas where such constructions and tourist screaming goes on, so most canopy tours are not about wildlife and ecology: they are about having fun. Zipping through the trees while suspended from a cable is certainly an experience to

Observing the Animals

Probably the greatest thrill in Costa Rica is the chance to **see wild animals** going about their daily business in the forest. If you spend some time in one or more of the parks and preserves, your chances of seeing some critters are good. However, some animals are much more easily seen than others, and some visitors have unrealistic expectations.

Ring-tailed **coatis** (locally known as *pizotes*) are frequently seen, and they are friendly and fun. **Monkeys** are everyone's favorites, and they are pretty common (a little too common, say the owners of stolen sunglasses and hats). Costa Rica has four species of monkeys: spider monkeys, white-faced capuchins, howler monkeys, and the rare squirrel monkeys (called *titís*).

We'd all love to see a **wild cat**, and Costa Rica has several species, including pumas, jaguars, ocelots, margays and jaguarundis. Outside of a zoo or rehabilitation center, however, you're unlikely to spot one of these secretive, nocturnal predators.

If you really want to see some of the rarer forest denizens, visit one of the more **remote parks, walk quietly,** and take your hikes in the **early morning or just before dusk.** I highly recommend hiring a local guide, who can show you animals (and plants) that you would never see on your own.

treasure, and such experiences are available in most parts of the country.

Fishing
Fishing in Costa Rica is simply spectacular. The most hard-core fishing fanatic or the casual angler can't fail to be impressed with catches of more than 15 sailfish in one day, tarpon well over 100 pounds, snook over 15 pounds, and large hauls of more exotic species such as machaca and roosterfish. Tico fishing guides have learned the value of this fishy profusion in attracting tourists, and are dedicated to catch-and-release. Most of the action takes place in the northern Caribbean region (for tarpon and snook) and off the Pacific coast (for billfish and other offshore species).

Diving
The Caribbean coast has substantial areas of coral reefs — still in surprisingly good condition in spite of pollution, earthquake damage and fishing pressure. The Pacific side is not known for great visibility, but if you want to get close to manta rays, sharks and other large pelagic species, this is one of the best places in the world to do so. **Cocos Island,** located a few hundred miles out in the Pacific, is a world-class diving destination that's famous for huge schools of scalloped hammerhead sharks.

Tropical River Cruises
One of the very best ways to get close to wildlife (without getting out of breath) is to take a **jungle cruise** along the spectacular canals of the northern Caribbean area or through the mangroves of the central or southern Pacific. Monkeys and crocodiles are close enough to touch (but don't).

Whitewater Rafting
A top global destination for whitewater rafting, Costa Rica offers several rivers suitable for all skill levels. The **Pacuare** and **Reventazón** are the two most popular. Outfitters pick up and drop off at San José hotels for one-day or overnight expeditions.

Windsurfing & Kiteboarding
With steady winds of up to 30 mph, **Lake Arenal** is one of the top kiteboarding and windsurfing locations in the world, and the

view is quite unique. Small lodges on the lakeside cater to all levels of skill.

Golf

Costa Rica has several championship courses, all with awesome mountain or ocean scenery. The Nicoya Peninsula boasts five spectacular seaside courses, all built in the 1990s by famous designers. Monkeys in the rough and crocodiles in the ponds add to the adventure.

Surfing

The movie *Endless Summer* highlights a few of the more spectacular surfing destinations in Costa Rica. The north Pacific region is famous for the tubular break at **Witches Rock**, and the southern Pacific region boasts one of the longest waves in the world (1/4 mile) at **Pavones**. On the Caribbean side, surfing is concentrated in the south near **Puerto Viejo** and **Cahuita**. The **Salsa Brava** is known to be a world-class surfing challenge. Board rentals and instruction are widely available. The killer breaks and the totally awesome surf scene attract gnarly surfers from all over the world, dude!

Volcanoes

With dozens of cones to choose from, few visitors to Costa Rica escape seeing a volcano, sometimes in all their erupting glory. Easy to get to, bubbling hot **Poás** is just outside San José. The perfect cone of **Arenal** attracts thousands of visitors to its rain forest-shrouded slopes. **Rincón de la Vieja National Park** has nine cones and a huge variety of volcanic terrain.

Taking the Kids

Ticos love kids. Kids love the beach and anything to do with monkeys. Almost all of the most visited areas of the country have dozens of organized tours and activities appropriate for the whole family. The food and water are good and most restaurants have the chicken tenders and fried potatoes that kids love.

Tico Cuisine

Restaurants aimed at tourists are not cheap — expect to pay about what you would in North America or a bit more. Typical Costa

Costa Rica Facts

Location:	Central America, between Nicaragua and Panama
Population:	4,075,000
Government:	Democratic republic
Languages:	Spanish, English (in Caribbean region), Indian languages
Highest Point:	Cerro Chirripó, 12,500 feet
Coastline:	Caribbean, 132 miles; Pacific, 635 miles
Biodiversity:	230 mammal species, 877 bird species, 220 reptile species, 180 amphibian species, 35,000 insect species, 9,000 plant species
Life Expectancy:	77 years
Literacy:	96%
Poverty rate:	18%
Economy:	Agriculture: 8.8%, Industry: 29.9%, Services: 61.4%

Rican restaurants are much less expensive and serve the same chicken, pork, beef, and fantastic seafood found in upscale tourist joints. Some of the lodges serve delightful dishes made from the freshest local seafood, vegetables and fruits. The level of hygiene is generally high, and upset stomachs from eating in local eateries are rare.

3. THE WILDLIFE OF COSTA RICA

If you love the natural world, and would like an opportunity to observe tropical animals and plants in their natural habitat, then Costa Rica is the place for you. Because of its location and geography, Costa Rica has an **astounding variety of wildlife.** Because of the people's wise decisions, they have managed to preserve far more of this wealth in its natural state than have most countries.

Within the borders of this small nation are hundreds of mammal, bird, reptile, and amphibian species; tens of thousands of insect species; and countless thousands of plant species (and this is just what's been described so far: when it comes to plants and small invertebrates, there are thought to be thousands more that scientists haven't gotten around to classifying yet).

With **dozens of national parks, refuges and reserves** of various kinds, the critters have plenty of space to roam around, and you are welcome to pay them a visit. Much of the tourist industry is built around showing off the country's natural wonders. Dozens of wilderness lodges and tour operators are at your disposal to help you get a glimpse of those exotic animals and plants.

At most parks, you're welcome to wander about on your own, but it's well worth the money to **hire a local guide** (which you can do at park ranger stations or through your lodge). With a guide,

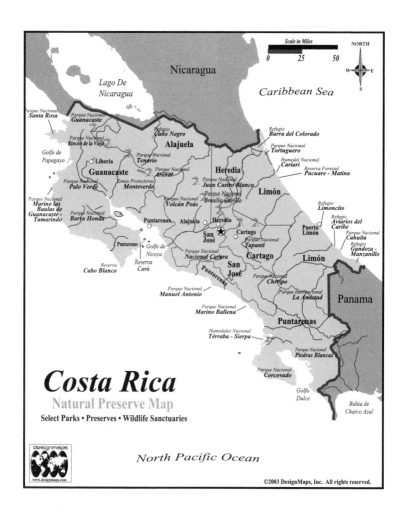

you'll learn much more about the local ecosystem, and probably see animals you would never have seen on your own. At some parks, going with a guide is your only option, as some are accessible only by boat, and a few restrict access to protect the animals.

Costa Rica has many different habitats, including rain forest, cloud forest, dry forest, marshes and mangrove swamps. Each has its own unique ecosystem, and its own set of inhabitants. For various reasons, some animals are much more commonly seen than others. To increase your chances of animal sightings, walk quietly in the forest, and take your hikes in the early morning or just before dusk, when animals are more active. I highly recommend hiring a local guide, who can point out animals that you would never see on your own. Sloths, for example, are hard to spot unless you know what you're looking for — to you or I, they tend to look like a lump of moss on a branch.

Here are some of the wild creatures you may hope to see, starting with the most common.

Mammals

The **ring-tailed coati** (*nasua nasua*), which the Ticos call a *pizote* (pronounced pee-SOH-tay), is a cute and gregarious creature with a long tail and a prehensile nose, which it uses to snuffle among the leaf litter on the forest floor for bugs, small lizards and frogs.

You're almost certain to see at least a few *pizotes*, as they are quite common, diurnal (active during the day), and not particularly shy. *Al contrario*, at some of the more frequented parks, where people have been feeding them, you may be accosted by bands of them begging for goodies. Their antics can be amusing, but you really shouldn't feed them or any other wild animals.

Costa Rica also has **raccoons** (*procyon lotor*), the same as the familiar North American variety. They occupy much the same niche as the *pizotes*, but are active at night. Another commonly seen forest dweller is the **agouti**, which looks something like a large brown guinea pig.

Costa Rica has four species of monkeys, three of which are found throughout the country. The most common is the playful **spider monkey** (*ateles geoffroyi*). You may also see the **white-faced capuchin** (*cebus capucinus*). The large black **howler monkeys** (*alouatta palliate*) make a loud noise that sounds less like howling than like the barking of a large dog. Even if you don't see them, you're sure to hear them far off in the forest.

The smallest and most exotic primate is the **Central American squirrel monkey** (*saimiri oerstedii*), which the locals call *mono tití*. This furry little goblin lives only in a small swath of coastal habitat from around Quepos on the Pacific coast down into the northern bit of Panama. Manuel Antonio National Park and the Osa Peninsula are the places to see *titís*.

Sloths are not rare, but are tough to spot in the forest, at least without a local guide. There are two varieties, the two-toed (*choloepus hoffmanni*) and the three-toed (*bradypus variegatus*). Sloths spend most of their time in trees snoozing, inching along

branches at a snail's pace, and eating leaves. Ironically, their slow and sedentary ways protect them from predators. Apparently, it's not only humans who tend to mistake a sloth for a lump of moss on a branch. Manuel Antonio is stiff with sloths.

The very patient may catch a glimpse of some of the rarer mammals, including **tapirs**, **anteaters**, **peccaries**, **coyotes**, **foxes**, and the **tayra**, a sleek weasel-like carnivore. **River otters** are especially fascinating to watch. Small forest mammals range from exotic ones such as the **kinkajou** (*potos flavus*) to more mundane species such as **porcupines**, **armadillos**, **skunks** and dozens of species of rodents. There are eight species of **opossum** and well over 100 species of **bats**!

Costa Rica has no less than six wild cats. The kings of the jungle are the magnificent spotted **jaguar** (*panthera onca*) and the **puma**

(*puma concolor*), a tawny relative of the North American cougar and Florida panther. Smaller felines are the beautiful little spotted **ocelot** (*leopardus pardalis*) and **margay** (*leopardus wiedii*), with a third relative that bears the unimaginative name of **little spotted cat** (*leopardus tigrinus*). The slightly larger **jaguarundi** (*herpailurus yaguarondi*) looks like a strange cross between a bear and a cat.

The puddy-tats are fairly rare, mostly nocturnal, and very shy of people. Your chances of seeing one in the wild are almost nil, unless you spend a good bit of time at one of the more remote lodges. If you are lucky enough to see a feline, you will probably see it from behind, rapidly fleeing from your headlights, as I did one dark night in the Osa Peninsula. There are a number of small

Don't Overlook the Small Stuff

We all want to see something really cool, such as a large mammal or a particularly exotic bird. But this isn't a TV show, and the critters don't always perform on a schedule that's convenient for us. Don't obsess about trophy sightings so much that you miss the less glamorous, but fascinating, beauty all around. Trees, flowers, lush tropical greenery, fruits and spices, butterflies and all kinds of interesting bugs (take a night hike to see some really exotic creepy-crawlies) are easy to see, going about their daily business unnoticed by humans who rush by, searching for the elusive quetzal.

zoos (Zoo Ave in Alajuela) and rehabilitation centers (Hacienda Matambu, near Curú) where you can see captive cats.

Reptiles & Amphibians

Snappy saurians may make you think twice about swimming in the rivers. The bridge at Tárcoles, which you'll cross shortly before reaching the Pacific coast from San José, is famous for the

shoals of pointy-nosed **crocodiles** in the river below. You'll see the smaller **caimans** on almost any river boat ride.

There's a huge variety of snakes (130 species), including boa constrictors, the bright yellow eyelash palm pit viper, the **fer-de-lance** (or *terciópelo*), one of the world's deadliest snakes, and the **bushmaster**, the world's largest pit viper, which can grow to 10 feet long and is locally called *matabuey* (ox-killer)! Watch your step in the forest, but don't worry — snakebites are rare.

There's a variety of brightly-colored frogs, called **poison-arrow frogs** because the local Indians make poison arrows from them. According to legend, if you lick one you'll get high, but I'd stick to rum if I were you. Notable lizards include enormous green **iguanas**, and the

Jesus Christ lizard, named for its ability to "walk on water" by skipping quickly across the surface.

Birds

The variety of birds is simply amazing, and so is the number of people who come to Costa Rica for the sole purpose of seeing them (the birds, that is). As this small country has more bird species than most continents, birders (or *twitchers*, as the English call them) have plenty of opportunities to add species to their *life lists*. Only a true birder can understand the excitement of seeing LBBs (Little Brown Birds) such as the tinamou, pie-billed grebe, Audubon's shearwater, wedge-rumped storm petrel, fulvous-whistling duck, great potoo and buffy-crowned wood partridge.

Everyone, however, loves such flamboyant fliers as **toucans** (six species), **hummingbirds** (between 50 and 60 varieties, each more brightly colored than the last) and Costa Rica's iconic bird, the **scarlet macaw**. These very large members of the parrot family are, despite the name, arrayed in all the colors of the rainbow. You'll see them throughout the southern half of the country, munching out in the almond trees (their images you'll see everywhere, on t-shirts, fridge magnets *et al*). Some birds have attained mythic status, like the **trogon**, the **resplendent quetzal**, the **harpy eagle** and the **curassow**, a ground bird that looks something like a well-dressed turkey. At night, you may see one of the many stately species of owls. Coastal regions teem with majestic herons (including the rufescent tiger heron), egrets, ibises, storks, spoonbills, cormorants and other shorebirds.

Flora

Plant lovers will likewise be in Heaven. Here are thousands of exotic plant species. Visitors from subtropical climes will find familiar plants gone wild — have you ever seen a palm tree with a 10-foot diameter trunk and 30-foot-long fronds?

The tropical rain forest has many more species of trees than its temperate counterpart. Whereas a typical North American forest is dominated by only a few species of trees, Costa Rican forests have thousands. Many produce edible fruits or other useful products. A few are dangerous, like the manzanillo tree, locally called *el hinchador*, which has a caustic latex sap. Flowering trees such as the jacaranda add seasonal splashes of color.

Epiphytes (plants that grow on other plants) such as **orchids** (*orquídeas* [or-KEE-day-oss] in Spanish) and **bromeliads** occupy every available square inch in the dripping, humid cloud forest.

 There are over 1,500 species of orchids here, and the country is a major supplier to the garden trade. Costa Rica's national flower is the **purple orchid** (*cattleya skinneri*), a very gaudy variety that blooms mainly in March and April. Orchids are not so easy to view in the wild, as most grow high up in trees. Fortunately, there are plenty of opportunities to see them in botanical gardens.

In fact, if you're interested in plants of any kind, I highly recommend a visit to one of the **many botanical gardens** throughout the country. The species are all neatly labeled, and you'll learn a lot about fruit trees and other cultivated plants that you aren't likely to see in the rain forest. Hummingbirds and butterflies are frequent visitors. You can find a list of botanical gardens throughout the country at: www.mapcr.com/CostaRicaGardens.html.

Dozens of wild and crazy fruits are available, both whole and fresh-squeezed. Whether familiar fruits such as mangos, papayas and pineapples (which are much sweeter and juicier here than the mass-shipped varieties you find at the supermarket in Des Moines) or exotic varieties such as *mamotes, pejibayes, chiverres* and *carambolas*, I highly recommend trying them whenever offered. Quench your thirst with a *pipa*, a chilled green coconut with a straw inserted so you can sip the sweet milk. Kids love to chew on a stalk of sugar cane.

Marine Life
The magnificent menagerie doesn't end at the water's edge. **Sea lions** live on the rocky Pacific coast, and **manatees** in the mangrove estuaries of the Caribbean. Nine types of **dolphin** make

What is Ecotourism, Anyway?

Ecotourism is a term that you'll hear kicked around quite a bit on your travels in Costa Rica. Of course, most visitors to the country are here to enjoy the natural wonders, but does that make us all ecotourists? Does spending a couple of hours strolling through the forest with a herd of other Gringos make you an ecotourist? Or must you spend a week helping the students with their research at one of the remote biological stations (for example Eco Lodge San Luis, near Monteverde) to earn the title?

In fact, ecotourism is a state of mind, an ideal of sustainable, minimally invasive tourism that both visitors and those in the tourism industry should strive for (alas, both groups often fall far short of the ideal). Ecotourists leave no litter, don't feed or interfere with the animals, and consume nothing but products that are harvested in a sustainable manner. A true eco-lodge recycles and conserves, releases no waste into the environment, strives to use renewable energy, and generally tries to have as little impact on the natural habitat as possible.

Ecotourism is also about preserving a very important species called local workers. One of the central concepts of ecotourism is the idea that local people can make a better living by helping tourists enjoy the rain forest than they could by chopping it down. Good ecotourists patronize local businesses, and buy local products whenever possible.

The International Ecotourism Society defines ecotourism as "responsible travel to natural areas that conserves the environment and improves the well-being of local people." Their web site at www.ecotourism.org includes lists of environmentally friendly lodges and tour operators.

The Costa Rican Tourist Board rates hotels on a scale of one to five green leaves, based on how close they come to the ideal of sustainable tourism. Find out more at www.turismo-sostenible.co.cr.

their homes in Costa Rican waters, and several species of whales, including **humpback, sperm, killer** and **pilot whales,** visit from time to time.

There are seven sea turtle species in the world, and five of them nest on Costa Rica's beaches. Female sea turtles return year after year to the beaches where they were born, and lay their eggs in the sand. When the babies hatch, they scamper to the sea en masse.

Watching the turtles do their thing on the beaches has turned into something of a New Age religious ritual for some. The folks who make the yearly pilgrimage here during spawning season are quite different from the birder crowd, but are just as fanatical. The hottest turtle-worship spots are Tortuguero on the Caribbean coast, where **hawksbill, loggerhead, green and leatherback sea turtles** nest, and isolated Playa Nancite in Santa Rosa

National Park on the Pacific, one of the few known nesting sites for the rare **olive ridley.** See the regional sections to find out what time of year the turtles are laying.

Some of the most impressive ocean wildlife is to be seen beneath the surface. Costa Rica is considered one of the top advanced diving destinations in the world, not for the usual coral reefs, but rather for the large pelagic species that frequent her waters. The Caribbean coast has a few areas of coral reef (notably in Cahuita National Park and the Gandoca-Manzanillo National Wildlife Refuge), and the northern Pacific coast has some fine reefs as well. However, the main draw for divers is the chance to mingle with schools of **tuna, sea turtles,** giant **manta rays** and several species of **sharks,** including the huge but harmless whale shark and several species of potential man-eaters such as hammerheads and bull sharks. You may also get to swim with dolphins and, on rare occasions, whales.

Beautiful stretch of beach just south of Manzanillo
on the Pacific Coast

Hummingbird in mid-flutter!

Shop your heart
out in the
Central Valley

Blue Macaw

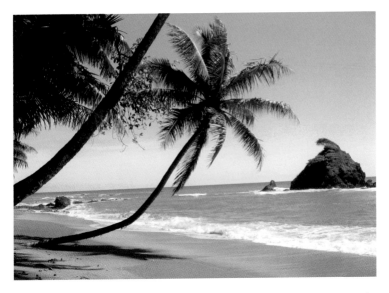

A slice of heaven: an empty beach in Corcovado National Park

Butterfly Farm

One of many stunning waterfalls in Costa Rica

Coastline south of Jacó, with Nicoya Peninsula in background

Northern Pacific big-fish hotspots are the Murciélago Islands (reached on dive charters out of Ocotal) and Santa Catalina Island (from Playa Flamingo). In the south, the best spots are around Caño Island, which you can visit on dive trips from the lodges at Drake Bay. See the Best Activities section for details of available dive trips.

This Pacific diving is advanced diving: deep dives far offshore, with rough seas and currents to contend with, to say nothing of the difficulty of keeping your composure around huge fish that could gulp you down like an olive.

The crown jewel of Costa Rican diving is **Cocos Island**, an uninhabited isle located a long 480-km boat ride southwest of the mainland, which Jacques Cousteau named as one of the most beautiful places in the undersea world. The entire island is a national park - it's covered by virgin forest and ringed by coral reefs. Here you may see all sorts of large pelagic species, including enormous schools of **scalloped hammerhead sharks**. The only way to get there is on a weeklong trip on one of two liveaboard dive boats.

Anglers haul in a vast variety of species. Familiar game species such as **sailfish, marlin, tuna, wahoo, jack, tarpon, snook, snapper, grouper** and **dorado** (the local name for the colorful and delicious fish also known as dolphin or mahi-mahi) are plentiful and large. Those with a taste for the exotic can target several types of **shark**, as well as a couple of fish found only in the region. The **roosterfish** is a large member of the jack family that's quite colorful, with a resplendent dorsal crest. Like all of its clan, it's a hard battler. Other local fish include the **machaca** and the freshwater **guapote**, a colorful little cichlid that's quite a fighter. Sawfish browse among the mud bottoms of the canals.

To learn more about Costa Rican wildlife, read the comprehensive *Costa Rica: The Ecotraveller's Wildlife Guide* by Les Beletsky; the pocket-sized *Costa Rican Wildlife: An Introduction to Familiar Species* by James Kavanagh; or *A Guide to the Birds of Costa Rica* by F. Gary Stiles. For those of a scientific disposition, **NatureServe** (www.natureserve.org/infonatura) has a searchable database of every species of bird, mammal, and amphibian found in Costa Rica (and neighboring countries).

4. SAN JOSÉ & THE CENTRAL VALLEY

For most visitors, Costa Rica's capital is a staging area for trips to the rain forests and the coasts. However, you're quite likely to end up staying at least one night in the area, as most flights to Costa Rica arrive late in the day, not leaving enough time to drive or fly to another part of the country. Why not make a virtue of necessity and have some fun?

Visit the **Central Market** and a couple of the city's small museums, and then take a trip to a **volcano** or a **coffee plantation**. In the evening, enjoy the amenities of the most cosmopolitan capital in Central America.

RECOMMENDED PLAN: Sleep at one of the nice hotels just outside of San José, and take day trips to some of the attractions of the Central Valley. If you have the energy, you can indulge in "multi-tours," catching two or even four attractions in one day! Stay in this region no more than a day or two, and then head for the coast or the rain forests.

Costa Rica's capital city is a sprawling metropolis — the greater urban area has over a million inhabitants. In Spanish colonial days, the capital was located in nearby Cartago, and San José was a sleepy village. Shortly after Costa Rica became independent from Spain in 1821, president Juan Mora Fernández moved the government to San José in order to symbolize a clean break with the past. Its comparatively recent history explains why San José has little in the way of grand colonial architecture (but suburbs such as Cartago, Heredia and Alajuela do). The local nickname for San José is *Chepe* (pronounced CHE-pe).

Don't try to drive around central San José, which features the usual Central American anarchy: treacherous potholes, very few street signs, and hordes of over-exuberant drivers on everything from tiny scooters to huge trucks to the odd mule cart.

Don't Miss...

- **Poás Volcano** — See a genuine bubbling volcano just a short ride from San José.
- **Coffee Plantation Tour** — See how much of the population of the Central Valley make their living, and where your morning cuppa comes from.
- **Zoo Ave** — At this delightful small zoo, not far from the airport, you can see all the animals you missed in the rain forest.

The local bus system is decent, so during the day it's practical to use it to get into town from your hotel. Better yet, taxis are cheap, and have the added benefit that you don't have to figure out how to get to where you're going. Local drivers are helpful, and usually know a smattering of English. At night, a taxi is the safest way to get around.

Once out of town, you should have no problems

driving—the main roads are generally well maintained. Do be sure to obtain a good map, however. You can rent a car right at the airport and get right on the Interamerican Highway, which runs the length of the country (it's also called Highway One north of San José, and Highway Two to the south).

ONE GREAT DAY IN SAN JOSÉ

Stay at a nice hotel out in the green suburbs, and take a local bus into central San José for the morning. In one day you can see the few highlights Costa Rica's capital city has to offer, and still have time to explore the area outside San José's city limits as well.

Morning

The **Parque Central** (Central Park) is one of the main hubs for city buses, so let's head there. The small park is a refuge from the noisy, hectic city center. If it's a Sunday morning, you might catch an outdoor concert.

A couple of blocks down Avenida 2, the **Teatro Nacional** (National Theater) is a local landmark that people will probably tell you to see. It's interesting enough to merit a quick look if you're in the area. The Neoclassical facade, with its statues of Beethoven and allegorical figures such as Comedy, Tragedy, Dance, Music, and Fame, is reminiscent of the great opera houses of Europe, but the indoor paintings of the coffee and banana harvests, and the wonderful parquet flooring, are purely Costa Rican. Just across the street is the **Café Parisienne**, a welcoming little sidewalk café that makes the perfect San José people-watching spot.

Stroll north along the **Avenida Central**, which at this point is a pedestrian mall lined with small shops, department stores and fast food restaurants. Between Calles 3 and 5 is the **Plaza de la Cultura** (Plaza of Culture), a bit of a park with a museum where you can see a nice collection of pre-Columbian artifacts in gold and jade.

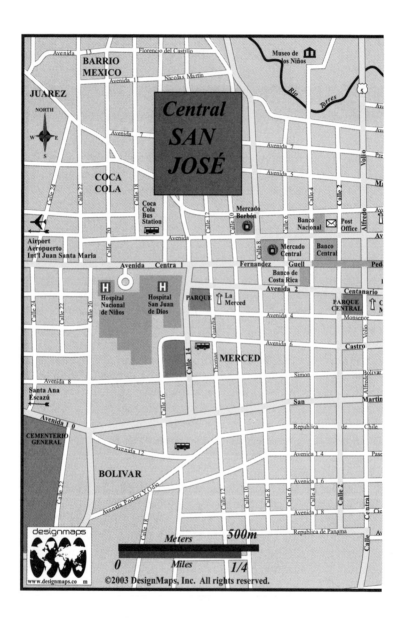

Central SAN JOSÉ

BARRIO MEXICO

JUAREZ

NORTH

COCA COLA

Coca Cola Bus Station

Airport Aeropuerto Int'l Juan Santa Maria

Avenida Centra 1

Hospital Nacional de Niños

Hospital San Juan de Dios

PARQUE La Merced

MERCED

Avenida 8

Santa Ana Escazú

Avenida 1 0

CEMENTERIO GENERAL

Avenida 12

BOLIVAR

Avenida Pochet Y Odio

Florencio del Castillo

Nicolas Martin

Museo de los Niños

Rio Torres

Avenida 7

Avenida 5

Mercado Borbón

Banco Nacional

Post Office

Mercado Central

Banco Central

Fernandez Guell

Banco de Costa Rica

Avenida 2

Centanario

PARQUE CENTRAL

Monsenor

Avenida 4

Castro

Avenida 6

Simon

San

Republica de Chile

Avenida 1 4

Avenida 1 6

Avenida 1 8

Republica de Panama

Meters 500m

0 Miles 1/4

Also on this square is the headquarters of the **Costa Rican Tourist Board**, where you can get travel information, maps and brochures on adventures throughout the country. Just around the corner, the **Pre-Columbian Gold Museum** and the **Fidel Tristan Jade Museum** are each worth a quick look.

If you walk east along Avenida Central a few blocks, you will come to a shopping area with stalls selling a complete array of tourist trinkets, toucans and t-shirts. *Info:* Costa Rican Tourist Board, open Mon-Fri 9am-5pm. Pre-Columbian Gold Museum, Avenida Central and Calle 5. Tel. 243-4202, open daily 9am-4:30pm. Fidel Tristan Jade Museum, Calle 9 and Avenida 7. Tel. 223-5800, open Mon-Fri 8:30am-3pm. $2.

A few blocks from the Plaza of Culture, up the hill called the Cuesta de Moras, is the **Bellavista Fortress** (look for the bullet holes, a legacy of the 1948 civil war). This impressive colonial fortress towers over the city and houses the **Muséo Nacional** (National Museum). Here you'll find another collection of fine pre-Columbian art objects, as well as pottery and jewelry from every region of the country, exhibits depicting events in Costa Rican history, and a butterfly garden. *Info:* National Museum, between Avenida Central and Avenida 2. Tel. 257-1433. Open Tue-Sat 8:30am-4:30pm; Sun 9am-4:30pm. $4. www.museocostarica.go.cr.

It's getting towards time for lunch, so let's head for the **Mercado Central** (Central Market), at Calle 6 and

Safety Tips

San José has its share of pickpockets — and that means plenty! An internal money belt (the kind that fits under your shirt) is a good idea. An external "fanny pack" is a very bad one — an irresistible temptation for thieves. Keep your eyes open, especially in the crowded streets around the Central Market.

Crooks aren't the only hazard to watch out for. **Sidewalks are in poor repair** in San José (and other cities), so watch your step. And be very careful crossing streets — drivers tend to have little regard for pedestrians.

Avenida 1. This bustling indoor market is a maze of stalls selling local crafts, clothing, flowers, meat, fish, vegetables, tropical spices and every little thing a Tico or a tourist might need. Also in here are several little *sodas* (cafés) where you can grab an inexpensive and tasty lunch, perhaps a *casado* with fish, rice and beans.

¿Y para tomar? To drink? Exotic **fruit smoothies** are popular in Costa Rica and are often served with lunch. Stop by a little stall and cool down with a glass of mango, papaya or piña (pineapple), or just point to the most brightly-colored jug.

San José Zoo–Skip It!

Although it has recently had some slight improvements, the zoo in San José, near Barrio Amón, is sad. The few animals seem listless in their small and dirty surroundings. New management is expected to clean things up but it will take millions to make the zoo something to be proud of. Perhaps the city should close it completely.

The excellent local **coffee** is available any time. Don't miss tasting one of Costa Rica's delicious beers. **Imperial** is tasty without being overpowering. **Bavaria Negra** is a robust dark beer.

Afternoon

In the afternoon, head out to **Alajuela**, one of the most pleasant of San José's many suburbs, near the airport (Alajuela is also a convenient and enjoyable place to find a hotel — see *Best Sleeps*). The main square is shaded by mango and palm trees, and surrounded by some splendid but faded colonial-era mansions. If you look closely, you may see some of the resident two-toed sloths (and possible some slothful humans lying about).

Just outside Alajuela, along the highway to Atenas, is the **Zoo Ave**, which is dedicated to reintroducing rehabilitated endangered species to the wild, particularly scarlet macaws. The large park is home to over 100 bird species and dozens of mammals and reptiles. In contrast to the San José city zoo, it is modern, clean and neat. The animals roam around in large, semi-open enclosures and little signs tell you the names of the tropical plants that fill the park.

You can get very close (almost too close at times) to monkeys (all 4 native species), pumas, tapirs, toucans, parrots (13 species) and other tropical creatures. Zoo Ave is well worth a visit, either at the beginning or end of your trip. I stop by over and over again.

This is a great place to visit with kids. It's also an especially nice spot for photographers, who can get shots of many forest denizens with no intervening bars or fences. Scarlet macaws pose regally and monkeys cavort.

Tip: Don't hang around directly under a tree with monkeys in it. Stand a few feet out of the drop zone, and you may get a good laugh, not only at the apes, but at the hapless tourists who didn't read this book! *Info:* **Zoo Ave.** www.zooave.org. Tel. 433-8989. Open daily 9am-5pm. Admission $15.

Evening
You'll have no problem finding a nice place to eat. San José has a nice variety of restaurants, offering French, Italian, Swiss, Spanish, Mexican and Asian cuisine, not to mention some great seafood. The better ones are priced about the same as in the US (see *Best Eats*).

Escazú is a suburb of San José popular with expatriates, where you can find all the US chain restaurants such as Outback, Pizza Hut

Find Your Way in San José

Ticos seldom use street addresses as such. Instead, locations are described as "on the corner of..." or "in between..." particular streets. In San José (and several other cities), *calles* (streets) run north-south, and *avenidas* (avenues) run east-west. Many, perhaps most, streets don't have street signs, so you may have to look for a street that does have a sign and count back (or forward) to the one you want.

and the burger joints. Out here you'll also find a few nice hotels like the **White House** and **Hotel Alta** that have wonderful restaurants open to the public.

San José's nightlife is quite a scene, with a full palette of bars and clubs, many featuring live music (see *Best Nightlife*). Of particular interest is the **Jazz Café** in San Pedro, which has good food and a nightly lineup of local and Central American performers. Do not walk around central San José at night. Take a taxi.

Risqué Nightlife

San José is famous for sex tourism. Certain bars and clubs teem with freelance (licensed and inspected) ladies of the night trolling for tourists with cash to spend on a pretty girl. So-called **Gringo Gulch** is the center for this type of action. The cornerstone is the interesting **Hotel del Rey** and the **Blue Marlin Bar** in its lobby (see *Best Sleeps*). As in most of the world, prostitution is legal and regulated by the authorities. Having sex with anyone under 18, however, is strictly illegal.

A FANTASTIC WEEKEND IN THE CENTRAL VALLEY

If you have two or three days to spend in the San José area, use it as a base for visiting the attractions of the surrounding area. It's preferable to stay in the quieter, more wholesome suburbs or just outside San José, as the city center has few attractions or activities that are likely to occupy you for more than one day.

The **Central Valley** has dozens of tours and excursions to choose from, lasting from an hour or two visiting a coffee plantation to overnight trips for rafting, fishing or cloud forest exploration. Short trips to more remote parts of the country are also feasible, thanks to small planes and an extensive network of landing strips, but you really needn't travel far from San José to see volcanoes and rain forests, or get into various adventure sports.

Most tour operators can include transportation to and from your hotel door.

Almost any hotel will help you book tours. You can, of course, book tours directly on your own or use one of the agencies I like: **Costa Rica Expeditions** in downtown San José (www.costaricaexpeditions.com; Tel. 257-0766, 222-0333), or **Costa Rica Outdoors** in Santa Ana (www.costaricaoutdoors.com; Tel. 282-6743, 282-6214, 800/308-3394 US).

Many companies offer **combination tours**. You can combine a visit to a volcano with a visit to a butterfly farm, followed by a tour of a coffee *beneficio,* or processing plant, with a stop somewhere for lunch. These combinations are a great idea, although some of the more strenuous activities, such as rafting, may leave you ready for a cold drink, dinner and bed at an early hour.

Rafting

One-day or overnight rafting trips on the **Pacuare** and **Reventazón** rivers are a great way to get out of town, see the rain forest, and get your adrenalin going. Outfitters such as **Costa Rica Expeditions** (see above) and **Ríos Tropicales** (www.riostropicales.com; Tel. 233-6455) specialize in rafting and organize everything, picking you up at your hotel in the morning and taking you to the put-in point in small tourist buses. Their rustic riverside lodges cook up hearty meals.

Either river can be covered in a one-day tour, but going overnight gives you a little more time on the river, and a chance to enjoy the tropical forest surroundings that tend to go by in a blur when you're racing through the rapids. Yes, you will get wet, but dry bags are provided so you can protect certain belongings. You won't need much more than a change of clothes.

Poás Volcano National Park

Just outside of town, **Poás Volcano National Park** is easy to get to, and well worth a look. The 2,708-meter volcano is quite active, although the last major eruption took place in 1954.

This is probably Costa Rica's most easily accessible volcano. You can drive almost to the rim itself and walk the rest of the way on a paved pathway. You can't go around the crater more than a short way, but there is a nice observation platform, and there is almost always some bubbly action going on.

Poás is one of the few volcanic craters in the world you can get to without getting out of breath. It is only a short walk on a nice smooth path from the car park to the crater rim. You will probably see a few *pizotes* cadging handouts. Don't fall for their pitch: just keep on walking and try not to let them catch your eye. There is also a small crater lake you can see after a walk through the forest, but go for the walk itself — the lake is a mild attraction.

Be sure you schedule your trip to Poás for **early in the morning,** as clouds start to move in and obscure the view of the crater as early as 10am. The visitor center is worth a look and you can, of course, get a nice cup of coffee. Try the tamales. They have the same toucan fridge magnets here that they have anywhere, so you may as well go ahead and buy here if you see something you like. *Info:* The visitor center is open 8am-4pm, and has a small cafeteria and souvenir shop. Entrance fee $7. Tel. 482-2165.

Poás Bubbling Over?

Occasionally the park is closed due to too much bubbly action. In 2006 Poás was going through a stage of mild activity, blorping out gobs of extremely hot mud and gases in the general direction of the viewing platform usually occupied by gawking tourists. **Call ahead** to avoid disappointment or scalding.

Coffee Tours

Two coffee farms and processing plants (known as *beneficios*), **Britt** and **Doka,** are open to the public and offer organized tours. Both are just outside San José, and either one would make a great visit to combine with a trip to Poás or to the waterfalls. A trip to a *beneficio* is a *must do* for all visitors to Costa Rica.

Café Britt is the big name in coffee in Costa Rica, and visitors see it advertised, served and sold everywhere. Cute little bags of their interesting coffee are on offer to tourists wherever they roam. The java is excellent, and the tour of their facilities just outside Heredia is informative and entertaining.

Coffee is the world's second-most traded commodity (after oil). The coffee trade is important not only for local communities in countries such as Costa Rica, but also for the global environment, as rain forest is often cleared to make space for coffee plantations (to say nothing of its importance in getting millions of people up in the morning).

Coffee beans require extensive processing before they're ready to brew up a cup (no, you can't pick your own beans and brew a shot on the spot). The tour shows you each step of the process, from planting to picking to classifying, peeling, soaking, fermenting, sun drying and roasting.

The Britt tour is noted for a twee, touristy flavor, but the flavor of their coffee is great. You can buy bags of coffee right there or later, perhaps at a slightly better price, in a local grocery store. *Info:* www.cafebritt.com. Tel. 260-2748. $20 for tour, $15 for transportation from most San José hotels.

In stark contrast, **Doka Estate**, located outside Alajuela near Sabanilla, wholesales almost all of their carefully crafted production directly to Starbucks, and operates a quieter, more informative tour of their fields and traditional processing operations.

Doka routinely kicks Britt's butt in the annual coffee tasting competition, sometimes winning both first place for their top-quality beans, and taking second place with their second-quality beans, beating everyone else's first-quality beans!

You can order coffee on the tour and have it shipped home. It's actually fairly economical to buy coffee this way and have it shipped back. You'll pay more at home for regular old coffee! *Info:* www.dokaestate.com. Tel. 449-5152. $15.

Both companies' tours are good. You need to call ahead to confirm opening times. Britt has "shows," and herds visitors through the place in groups, so it's probably best to find out when the show times are before dropping in.

Lankester Gardens

These 27-acre gardens were founded by British naturalist Charles Lankester West in 1917, and are now run by the University of Costa Rica. Here you'll find an enormous collection of native species, including **nearly a thousand varieties of orchids**, as well as bromeliads, heliconias, palms, bamboo and other trees. Hummingbirds and butterflies are everywhere.

Nice **paved trails** make it easy to wander about the gardens and forests, which represent several distinct ecosystems, each with its characteristic species of orchids. There's a small gift shop. This would be a great stop to combine with a visit to Irazú or one of the coffee plantations.

Life Outside Britt!

Many visitors never realize that the spectacular experience in coffee provided by Café Britt can be even more spectacular when provided by other great Costa Rican brands like Volio or Tres Generaciones (Doka). Café Rey is another high-quality brand. They all offer a variety of roasts such as dark, espresso, breakfast blend, selecto, European blend, etc.

The best place to buy coffee in Costa Rica is in any old grocery store. Duty free shops at the airport are not any cheaper and the selection in grocery stores is much better.

Info: **Lankester Gardens** is located in Paraíso de Cartago, 6 km from Cartago. Open 9am-3:30pm daily. Entry $5 adults; $1 kids. Tel. 552-3247.

Heliconia Island

This **private botanical garden** is smaller and less comprehensive than Lankester, but it's very well designed and is worth a visit, especially if you love flowers and/or bananas. Architect and graphic designer Tim Ryan laid out the five-acre gardens on an island in the Puerto Viejo river.

The namesake **heliconia** is a lovely tropical flower. Here are **70 different species** from all over the world, at least some of which are blooming year-round. The garden also features a huge variety of orchids, bromeliads, ferns, philodendrons, fruit trees, and some very rare palms. You can taste several varieties of bananas. The region has **over 400 bird species**: you may see not only rain forest denizens such as parakeets, trogons, toucans and tanagers, but water birds such as herons, egrets, kingfishers and kiskadees. Of course, hummingbirds and butterflies are abundant. *Info:* **Heliconia Island** is located 8 km from Puerto Viejo de Sarapiquí, about an hour north of San José. There's an elegant restaurant. www.heliconiaisland.com. Tel. 397-3948.

La Paz Waterfall Gardens

Not too far from Poás, **La Paz Waterfall Gardens** has five spectacular waterfalls, which you can admire from an easy walking trail. A frothing white waterfall in the midst of lush green vegetation is one of the most photogenic scenes known to man. This large tourist park also has several other attractions. There's an enormous enclosed structure with over 4,000 butterflies flitting about (they claim it's the **largest enclosed butterfly garden in the world**, and I believe it). The hummingbird garden is also quite amazing, featuring 24 different species of these fascinating little aerobats. There are 3.5 km of walking trails, orchid houses, a small restaurant and a gift shop.

La Paz is not a cheap thrill, and it is far from undiscovered. But if you don't mind sharing the peace and quiet with a few busloads of other tourists, it makes a good visit to combine with other nearby attractions such as Poás or one of the coffee tours. Kids especially love the butterflies, some of which they can touch.

Info: La Paz Waterfall Gardens, www.waterfallgardens.com. Tel. 482-2720. Open 8:30am-5:30pm. Adults: $25; children 12 and under: $15. There's also a hotel, called Peace Lodge, which has luxurious designer rooms that start around $195 double. www.waterfallgardens.com/lapaz-peacelodge.htm. Tel. 225-0643.

A WONDERFUL WEEK IN THE CENTRAL VALLEY

If you can spend a week in the San José area, as in the weekend plan, use it as a base for visiting even more of the Central Valley: volcanoes, parks, gardens, and coffee towns await!

Irazú Volcano

In 1963, while President Kennedy was on a visit, Costa Rica's highest volcano, **Irazú**, blew its stack, sending clouds of muddy ash all over San José and the Central Valley. This kind of thing is said to be good for the coffee crop. At 3,432 meters (11,260 feet), it is still active from time to time and, although not quite as easy to get to as Poás, it is worth a visit if you fancy seeing what the surface of the moon looks like (according to astronaut Neil Armstrong). There are **four craters** to gaze at, and a **bright green lake**.

This is another attraction that you need to get to early in the morning, due to developing morning cloud cover. If the day is very clear (a rare occurrence) and you hold your mouth right, you might just be able to see both the Caribbean and Pacific coasts from up top. If Poás is closed due to too much bubbly activity, and you really, really want to see a bubbling crater, then Irazú is the thing to do, and is actually just as nice a trip. *Info:* **Irazú Volcano National Park**. The visitor center has a small restaurant, and is open 8am-4pm. Tel. 551-9398.

Heredia

In spite of seeming a bit busy and run-down, **Heredia** is actually a small hub of middle-class and university students contributing to a **lively club and restaurant scene**. It is halfway between the airport and downtown San José, and on the way to Poás Volcano and the coffee *beneficios*. Above Heredia, **Debbie King's Country Inn** (see *Best Sleeps*), is a good place for an exploration base convenient to San José but high in the healthy hills overlooking the heaving city.

If you need overnight lodging convenient to the airport but out of the urban nastiness that is San José, Heredia is a good choice (see *Best Sleeps*). It's convenient to the airport and downtown, and it's close to major routes to both the Pacific and Caribbean coasts.

Braulio Carillo National Park, Volcán Barva

With two volcanoes and miles of tropical cloud forest, **Braulio Carillo National Park** is close to San José (12 miles), but usually overlooked by tourists in a hurry to get to Monteverde and the "crowd forest." If you have driven from San José to the Caribbean coast along the main route, you may remember passing through an area of mountains lush, lush, lush with tropical foliage, dripping wet. This is Braulio Carillo.

For quetzals, toucans, trogons, eagles, indeed **over 500 species of birds**, and the usual Costa Rican mix of mammals—monkeys, sloths, *pizotes* and maybe an ocelot—there is really no need to travel further. Every inch of space is covered with plants, including showy epiphytes such as orchids and bromeliads.

There are two ranger stations along the main highway, and each has **some good trails**. Another popular trail leads from the town of Sacramento to the crater of Volcán Barva, a dormant volcano, with several crater lakes.

The park is huge, at over 21,000 acres (47,000 hectares), with many trails, some of them for serious campers willing to spend up to four days hiking in the mist. Guides are available through the park or through local lodges. There is a lot of exploring to be done in this huge, but much-less-frequented cloud forest park. However, note that this park has an unfortunate **reputation for crime**. Always check in at the ranger station before setting out, and consider hiring a local guide – and do *not* leave valuables in your car. *Info:* Braulio Carillo National Park is about 20 km northeast of San José. Buses stop right in front of the ranger stations. The main station is just past the southern entrance to the park. Open Tue-Sun 8am-4pm. $15. Tel. 261-2619.

Busloads of tourists head for the **aerial tram**, just north of the park boundary. Here you can take pricey cable car rides through the forest canopy (www.rfat.com. Tel. 257-5961).

Centro Neotrópico SarapiquíS

Yes, the name of this place does have a capital 'S' at the end of its name! This **research and educational center** is run by a Belgian nonprofit organization, and includes a jungle lodge and three interesting attractions. The botanical garden has **over 400 native plants**, all neatly labeled, including epiphytes, orchids, ferns and various plants beloved of hummingbirds and butterflies. There's also a museum with exhibits on rain forest biology and the indigenous peoples of the region.

Unlike some of its neighbors to the north, Costa Rica doesn't have very many Pre-Columbian archaeological sites. Here you'll find one of the best in the country. A **15th-century indigenous village** has been excavated and partially reconstructed, and there are some cool stone statues and **petroglyphs**. *Info:* Just off the main road near the village of La Virgen de Sarapiquí, about 85 km from San José. www.sarapiquis.org. Tel. 761-1004. Rooms in the lodge run about $82-116 double.

5. THE NORTH CARIBBEAN COAST

The northern coastal region is low, with swampy, forested plains fronted by magnificent wild and dangerous sandy beaches. Hardcore anglers, turtle worshipers and birders indulge their fantasies.

Tortuguero and **Barra del Colorado** offer some of the best wildlife-viewing opportunities in the country. You can see monkeys and sloths, crocs and caimans, as well as over 450 bird species, from the comfort of a small boat.

RECOMMENDED PLAN: Divide your time between one of Barra del Colorado's tarpon-and-snook camps and one of Tortuguero's lagoon-side wildlife lodges. Let your lodge arrange transportation from San José or wherever.

A **labyrinth of canals, marshes, wetlands and rain forest** extends for miles and miles inland from the coast, a vast tangle of trees, vines, orchids, fish, birds and monkeys. There are **no roads to speak of** in this region. You'll arrive here by small plane, and get around by water taxis.

The **Barra del Colorado** area, to the north near the border with Nicaragua, is famous for fishing, while **Tortuguero** to the south is known as a place to observe wildlife. However, the entire region is splendid territory for both pursuits: excellent fishing charters are available at Tortuguero-area lodges, and Barra del Colorado Wildlife Refuge is even more remote than Tortuguero National Park.

Don't Miss...

• **Tortuguero National Park** — Cruise through the jungle, looking in on the watery activities of caimans, turtles, monkeys, sloths and birds, birds, birds! Turtle worship on the beach at night — very New Age.
• **Barra del Colorado** — Just a few hundred feet offshore, you can battle with tarpon well over a hundred pounds, until your arms give out. Then cruise the canals for fat snook and local species such as machaca.

Area Map of
Northern
Caribbean

ONE GREAT DAY ON THE NORTH CARIBBEAN COAST

The Caribbean coast is a bit far from San José for day trips, but never fear. You can get in and out of this region in just one day.

Tour operators can arrange small buses from your San José hotel to the coast to link up with jungle cruises through the canals of **Tortuguero National Park** and bring you back again the same day, exhausted, but just in time for milk and cookies.

Day trips from cruise ships docking at Limón usually run north up the canals on jungle tours and back again in time for shrimp cocktails. If you are staying in one of the Caribbean hotels you can indulge in short trips inland to the rain forest or along coastal canals to gape at wildlife or fish.

Rafting on a wild class IV river is easy to arrange from the south Caribbean area. **Costa Rica Expeditions** and **Ríos Tropicales** are the most experienced rafting tour operators, and both offer one- or two-day trips for all levels of skill. Both companies have overnight facilities in the rain forest at the edge of the river. *Info*: Costa Rica Expeditions: www.costaricaexpeditions.com; Tel. 257-0766, 222-0333. Ríos Tropicales: www.riostropicales.com; Tel. 233-6455.

A FANTASTIC WEEKEND ON THE NORTH CARIBBEAN COAST

A quick overnight trip to the coast to wrestle with tarpon and snook is quite feasible. Flights from San José usually run early in the morning, so you can easily get in a whole day of fishing on the first day of a weekend trip.

Fishing in Barra del Colorado
The lodges in both **Parismina** and **Barra del Colorado** (see *Best Sleeps*) are attuned to what anglers want: they pick you up

planeside, hustle your bags to your room and get you out on the water quickly and comfortably. If you plan your weekend carefully, you can get in two full days of tarpon bashing, and be back in San José Sunday evening ready for *un zarpe*, a nightcap.

A weekend enjoying Costa Rica's north Caribbean coast begins by catching an early half-hour flight out of San José to Barra del Colorado. Have your camera ready in the plane because, if it's not raining too hard, you can get some good pictures of the lodges and inlet as the plane makes its approach to the tiny runway.

There are only three lodges in the area, and they are all serious centers of fishing, fishing, and fishing. The people who stay at these lodges spend all day fishing and all night drinking and lying about fishing. People who tease birders for being intense have never stayed at a big-time fishing lodge.

Costa Rica's Best Fishing

Costa Rica has so many great fishing opportunities, it's tough to narrow things down. But for truly world-class, trip-of-a-lifetime fishing, two fisheries stand out: tarpon and snook on the Caribbean, and billfish on the Pacific.

The **Barra del Colorado** area, on the Caribbean, has **monstrous tarpon** in the rivers and just offshore, and excellent action for snook and exotic local species in the canals. Take your pick of several excellent fishing lodges.

The **Pacific coast is billfish territory**: catches of a dozen sailfish in one day are not unusual. **Quepos** is the largest sport-fishing center in the country, but just about any place on the Pacific can be a starting point for a classic fishing trip. **Playa Flamingo** in the north and **Puerto Jiménez** in the south are also prime fishing destinations.

Silver King Lodge, **Río Colorado Lodge** and **Casa Mar** are the choices. I love all three lodges, the owners and the people who run them. All are comfortable, with memorable food, lots of jungle character, top-quality equipment and sharp guides. Their prices are similar. You will probably catch the same amount of

Snook for Supper

If you love fish, don't pass up the chance to try **snook**, a delicious light white fish. In the US, snook is classified as a game species, so it's not available at restaurants or markets. In Costa Rica, however, snook are plentiful, and you're certain to see some on the table, especially in the Caribbean region.

fish no matter which lodge you stay at. The success of your fishing trip depends more on luck, time of year, and weather than on which lodge you sleep in.

The fishing here is simply spectacular. The fish are large, plentiful and easy to catch. **Tarpon** swarm in their thousands off the river mouths. Offshore, anglers haul in tarpon over 150 pounds on a daily basis, as well as large **jack** and **wahoo**. In the rivers, you'll catch snook over 25 pounds, smaller tarpon, **snapper**, **sharks** and exotic local species such as **machaca** and **calba**. If you've a taste for the unusual, you can even catch a **sawfish**.

The lodges are **all-inclusive**, so you don't have to worry about restaurants or bars. Wine, beer, rum, and in some cases all drinks, are unlimited, and tables groan under enormous dinner buffets. There is little doubt in my mind that some of the best eating in the entire country goes on in the dining rooms of the three lodges in Barra del Colorado. It's possible to take **jungle tours** or indulge in **spa treatments** at most of the lodges, if for some reason you don't want to spend every available daylight hour fishing. *Info:* Silver King Lodge: www.silverkinglodge.com; Tel. 381-1403, 381-0849, 800/847-3474 US. Río Colorado Lodge: www.riocoloradolodge.com; Tel. 232-4063, 232-8610, 800/243-9777 US. Casa Mar: www.casamarlodge.com; Tel. 433-9287, 433-8834, 800/543-0282 US.

Tortuguero

For family members who may not be power anglers, **Tortuguero** has several lagoon-side lodges such as **Laguna Lodge** and **Tortuga Lodge**, offering comfort and proximity to **Tortuguero National Park**. A jungle cruise in a small boat is one of my favorite ways to get out in the rain forest to view birds, monkeys, crocs, and other interesting wildlife. The canals and creeks around the park are a wonderful place to get very remote, very quickly and comfortably. Kids love it too, and the lodges have pools to keep them busy during umbrella-drink hours.

The wild and spectacular beaches of the northern Caribbean side are the nesting grounds of **green, leatherback and hawksbill sea turtles**. The park coordinates carefully controlled nighttime beach walks to see turtles nesting (from a respectful distance). Opportunities to volunteer to help the turtles can be arranged quickly for short or long terms. *Info:* Contact the **Caribbean Conservation Corps** (www.cccturtle.org; Tel. 224-9215) to find out more.

Tortuguero is also a prime area for tarpon and snook fishing, and is the base of the coast's most famous and respected independent guide, **Captain Eddy Brown**, with his 19-foot center console, twin Yamaha **Bull Shark** (Tel. 383-6097, 382-3350). Book well in advance, as he is quite popular. He'll come and pick you up at your lodge and provide everything you need except sunscreen and muscle power for cranking in the over-100-pound tarpon common in the area.

A WEEK ON THE NORTH CARIBBEAN COAST

A week on the Caribbean coast gives you plenty of time to enjoy the beaches, the fishing and the wildlife. Spend three or four days at one of the lodges in the **Barra del Colorado** area: Silver King, Río Colorado, or Casa Mar (see *Best Sleeps*). Then take a water taxi to Tortuguero to stay at one of the canal-side lodges: Laguna Lodge or Tortuga Lodge. Spend the mornings touring nearby **Tortuguero National Park** by small jungle boat. After lunch, soak in the pool and possibly indulge in a siesta, then have a fine dinner with Concha y Toro Chilean wine and, after dark, take part in turtle worship on the beach.

TWO WEEKS ON THE NORTH CARIBBEAN COAST

If you're fortunate enough to have up to two weeks to spend in this region, you can enjoy four very different kinds of vacation experience, and please all members of the family (or you could simply spend more time pursuing your passion). Sample the fishing at **Barra del Colorado** and/or **Parismina**, then spend a few days cruising the jungle and turtle worshipping at **Tortuguero**, with plenty of time left over for **relaxing on the spectacular beaches** further down the Caribbean coast.

Tortuguero National Park

One of Costa Rica's most popular national parks, Tortuguero covers 77,000 acres and encompasses no less than eleven different habitats, including several types of rain forests, swamps, and lagoons, each with its own variety of plants and animals. The magnificent 22-mile beach is a favorite nesting ground for hawksbill, loggerhead, green and leatherback sea turtles.

There's no road access to Tortuguero. You'll arrive by boat from Parismina, or by small plane. Once here, you'll find the park delightfully accessible by small boat and on foot. There is one smallish hill, Cerro Tortuguero, but no mountains to stress hikers walking in the rain forest. Photographers and birders are especially drawn to the area since wildlife is relatively easy to get close to in the narrow, covered jungle tour boats.

For me, tours through the jungle by boat are the very best way to

see wildlife and enjoy the tropical rainforest. Hiking up and down mountains through the cloud forest is fine for some people, but I'll take sitting back in a small boat drifting through backwater creeks. Some of my best wildlife photography has been done on a jungle cruise in Tortuguero. Transportation, and tours to the park, are best arranged through your lodge (see *Best Sleeps*).

Tortuguero is famous for the **hawksbill, loggerhead, green** and **leatherback sea turtles** that come here to lay their eggs on the beach. In fact, the name of the park refers to a turtle hunter. In years past, *tortugueros* (turtle-hunters) stalked the green turtle almost to extinction, not only for meat but also for the supposed aphrodisiac qualities of their eggs.

In 1959, Dr. Archie Carr of the University of Florida founded a local organization to preserve sea turtles, and today the turtles' reproductive rites take place under the paternal gaze of man. No one is allowed on the beach unaccompanied at night, prime laying time, so you'll have to arrange for a guide (which you can do through your lodge) to watch mama turtle dig her nest in the sand or, if you are very lucky, to see the hatchlings scurry to the sea.

Hawksbill, loggerhead, and Pacific green turtles nest from July through October. The leatherback, the world's largest sea turtle, nests from February through July. Learn more about Costa Rica's sea turtles at www.costaricaturtles.com/turtles.html and www.cccturtle.org.

Inland from the beaches lies a labyrinth of freshwater canals and lagoons, inhabited by manatees, river otters, caimans, turtles, and over 50 species of freshwater fish, to say nothing of the monkeys, sloths and birds you'll see on the banks. *Info:* There are three park stations, all open 8am-4pm. **Cuatro Esquinas Headquarters** is in the town of Tortuguero, and features trails along the beaches. Camping is available. The **Sector Jalova Station** is further south, near Jalova Lagoon and the town of Parismina. On the western border of the park, **Aguas Frías Station** has a trail that leads to the highest point in the park at Lomas del Sierpe (1,000 feet). There's an entrance fee of $7.

Barra del Colorado National Wildlife Refuge
North of Tortuguero, along the border with Nicaragua, Barra del Colorado National Wildlife Refuge is even larger (at 200,000 acres, CR's second-largest rain forest preserve) and more remote. Like Tortuguero, most of the park is a maze of canals, creeks, sloughs, bayous and every sort of watery landscape, inhabited by crocs, caimans, manatees and the usual vast array of animals and birds.

Here you can get nose-to-nose with critters, with none of the crowds further south in Tortuguero. The refuge is accessible only by boat, so you'll need to arrange a tour through your lodge.

Barra del Colorado village is a cluster of run-down shacks with a colorful history that includes Nicaraguan refugees and gun- and drug-smugglers. Today it has few facilities other than the airstrip, and is of no particular interest to tourists. *Info:* Entrance to the refuge costs $5 per person, which you pay at the ranger station near the Silver King Lodge. There are no tourist facilities to speak of, but information is available at **Diana's Souvenirs** (Tel. 710-6592) in the village of Barra del Colorado.

Beaches
Beaches north of Limón are **wild, remote and dangerous**. Huge piles of driftwood stretch into the distance for miles. The surf is thunderous with heavy undertow. Bull sharks feed

Don't Feed the Monkeys!

Everyone loves monkeys, and in Costa Rica, it isn't hard to get a close-up look at their antics. Those cute little apes are rowdy characters, however, so use caution. At many remote lodges you may get a little too close. It's not unusual for the precocious primates to waltz right in through an open window and help themselves to food or unguarded belongings. In places where monkeys have been encouraged by tourists feeding them, they can get aggressive and may even bite. Watch your belongings, **don't try to pet them**, and whatever you do, **do not feed them**. Standing directly under monkeys in trees is also not recommended.

among the breakers. There are no beachfront restaurants or other facilities, except at a few of the Tortuguero-area lodges.

If you are a serious **beach hiker** you will love the north Caribbean beaches. If you are a regular old beach lover, then head for the beaches south of Limón, where you'll find safe swimming spots and plenty of places to get a cold beer.

6. THE SOUTH CARIBBEAN COAST

South of Limón you'll find spectacular beaches backed by mountains and more rain forest. The flavor is very Caribbean, with some locals speaking a Creole dialect of English and sporting dreadlocks. Surfing, snorkeling and hanging out on the beach are the main activities.

RECOMMENDED PLAN: Spend some time chilling out at one of the Rasta-flavored beach towns south of Limón, such as **Cahuita** or **Manzanillo**. Steer clear of Limón itself, a dirty and noisy port city. Explore the natural wonders of **Cahuita National Park**, both above and below the water. If time permits, visit the remote **Gandoca-Manzanillo National Wildlife Refuge**.

The southern part of Costa Rica's Caribbean coast is famous for a laid-back atmosphere and a little "Rasta" flavor. Hard-core fishing fans and wildlife enthusiasts tend to visit the northern Caribbean, whereas the travelers who come down south are mainly interested in beaches, partying, snorkeling and surfing. **Skip Limón** if at all possible. In spite of recent efforts to pretty things up for cruise ship visitors, it is a run-down, rough port town, unpleasant and hot. Fortunately there is a turnoff to the south at the edge of town, so you can drive right by and not bother with it at all.

South of Limón, the beaches are mostly black or gray sand with big rocks and coconut palms backed by mountains and dense rain forest. While the north is only accessible by small plane or boat (part of its charm), the south is tourist-friendly, with a reasonably well-paved road running from Limón to just past **Manzanillo**.

In this part of Costa Rica, Latin culture mixes with a more Caribbean flavor. Many of the locals are black folks who speak a **Creole** dialect of English, and cook in a more Caribbean style. Some sport dreadlocks. Occasionally there is the smell of herb.

Don't Miss...

• Manzanillo — Veg out at a groovy oceanside hotel, drink beer and eat fish at Maxi's. Check out the action on the beach from upstairs.
• **Snorkeling at Cahuita** — The beach is beautiful for swimming, and the coral reefs are not far from shore, making this one of the few places in Costa Rica where you can snorkel right from the beach.

The beaches are astoundingly pretty, with coconut palms, clear water and coral reefs. Surfing the **Salsa Brava** is a dream for hard-core surfers. **Cahuita** and **Puerto Viejo** are the spots for diving and snorkeling. Both these towns have plenty of tourist activities, laid-back bars, interesting restaurants with Caribbean spices and dance clubs for the energetic. Alternative youth culture festers in surfer enclaves.

Remember, Central America is not Europe. Most of Costa Rica's urban centers, including San José, Limón, Liberia and some of the smaller towns such as Quepos and Golfito, are generally dirty, noisy, choked with traffic, and not very safe places to be. Despite what other guidebooks may tell you, there is very little of touristic interest in any of the cities, unless you're really interested in decayed colonial architecture or sleazy bar culture.

You'll find better lodgings, better restaurants and a generally more relaxed and pleasant atmosphere, at jungle lodges and beach resorts outside of towns. And, after all, it's the jungles and beaches you're going to Costa Rica for, so why not spend your time close to the action?

ONE GREAT DAY ON THE SOUTH CARIBBEAN COAST

The south Caribbean coast is too far for a day trip from San José. If you're staying in this region, the **Aviarios del Caribe** private wildlife refuge makes a nice day trip. It's easy to visit in the morning, leaving the afternoon for lounging about on the beach.

Aviarios del Caribe
This privately-run wildlife refuge is on the coast just north of Cahuita, where the Estrella River meets the sea. It's the site of the **Buttercup Sloth Rescue Center**, created by Americans Judy and Luis Arroyo in 1991. If you like sloths, this is the place for you. You can visit Buttercup and the other residents at the rehabilitation center, and learn more about these gentle creatures (this is a great place to bring the kids).

Torguguero Canal

Boca Río Matina

Matina
· Estrada
Maravilla · Cocal Portete
Victoria Rio Blanco
32
Trébol
Asunción 247 Bomba

Area Map of
SouthernCaribbean

Limon

Refugio
Limoncito

Nicaragua

Limon

Panama

NORTH

Refugio
**Cuenca
del Rio
Banano**

*Parque
Internacional*
Amistad

Armenia · · Guaria · Cahuita

36

Parque Nacional
Cahuita

Rio Estrella

Reserva
Hitoy Cerere

Hone Creek

Bribri

Shiroles · Fields
Bratsi

Refugio
**Gandoca-
Manzanillo**

**Puerto
Viejo**
Manzanillo

Rio Telire

Rio Sixaola

Gandoca

· Telire

· Katsi

Daytonia

Sixaola

*Parque
Internacional*
Amistad

Kichuguecha

Alto
Lari
·

Purita

Panama

CORDILLERA

TALAMANCA

Rio Lari

*Parque
Internacional*
Amistad

designmaps
www.designmaps.com

©2003, 04 DesignMaps, Inc. All rights reserved.

Surf Spot

Sportfishing

Volcanic Park

National Park

Forest Reserve

Wildlife Refuge

Protected Zone

If you'd like to see sloths in their natural habitat, you can take a boat tour in the freshwater canals that wind through the wildlife sanctuary. You'll probably also see caimans, turtles, *pizotes*, and monkeys. The fortunate may be entertained by the antics of river otters or kinkajous. Over 300 bird species have been cataloged. There's also a nice easy walking trail. The lodge has seven rooms with private bath that start around $75 double (but no restaurant). *Info:* Aviarios is just off the main coast road about 31 km south of Limón. The Limón-Cahuita bus will stop right at the entrance if you tell the driver when you get on. www.ogphoto.com/aviarios. Tel. 750-0775. Boat tours are offered throughout the day, and cost $30 per person.

The Costa Rican Creoles

The area south of Limón is home to an ethnic group quite different from the Spanish-speaking Mestizos you'll meet elsewhere in the country. These black **Creoles**, who constitute about 3% of Costa Rica's population, are descendants of Jamaicans who immigrated here in the 19th century to work on the banana plantations. They speak a dialect of English similar to the Patois spoken in Jamaica, and cultural ties to the Anglophone Caribbean are strong. You'll notice a difference not only in the local language, but also in the cuisine, the music, the buildings and the general lifestyle. Cool breeze, man!

A FANTASTIC WEEKEND ON THE SOUTH CARIBBEAN COAST

This region is eminently doable as a weekend trip, but use a tour company; they can make arrangements to fly to the small airstrip south of Limón, then take a van to the interesting areas of the south coast. Heading down here on your own would mean either a fairly long drive from San José or a hassle finding ground transportation (the Limón airstrip has no car rental facilities), making it impractical for a two- or three-day trip.

Unlike the Nicoya area, the southern Caribbean coast has nothing that you could call a luxury resort, but there are plenty of modest but comfortable bed-and-breakfast-style lodgings in the area around Cahuita and Puerto Viejo, many on gorgeous beaches.

Choose a hotel close to the beach, like **Villas del Caribe**, southeast of Puerto Viejo, or **Cariblue Bungalows Hotel** on Playa Cocles (see *Best Sleeps*), and surrender yourself to the laid-back tropical lifestyle. Rise late in the morning and savor a cup of some of the finest coffee in the world. Spend the day lazily strolling along the beach, or pay a visit to Cahuita National Park. In the evening, drink a little rum and listen to some Reggae music.

There are several great restaurants where local seafood is superb. Of particular note is **La Pecora Nera**, southeast of Puerto Viejo, for an Italian angle on things with fresh, fresh, fresh fish; and the ultimate end-of-the-road beach bar, **Maxi's** at the end of the road in **Manzanillo** (see *Best Eats*). Sit upstairs to check out the beach action while sipping an Imperial. Try the whole snapper (*pargo entero*).

The area around Manzanillo is known as a destination for *Gringas* from North America and Europe who come for a romantic fling with a willing local.

Beaches

From Cahuita all the way down to Manzanillo, huge rocks and stands of coral punctuate endless expanses of gray and black sand. Coconut palms droop gracefully, shading funky little beach bars where locals and tourists go to seed at their own pace. The water is usually quite clear and Caribbean-blue, but still dangerous in places. You can snorkel, fish, surf or just drink.

Cahuita National Park

This park features 14 km of beaches backed by rivers, swamps and rain forest, as well as one of Costa Rica's few stretches of coral reef (sadly degraded from agricultural runoff and earthquake upheaval but still nice). At the beaches sheltered by the offshore reef, the water is calm and safe for swimming.

You can snorkel out to the reef, which is to the north off Puerto Vargas, but for serious diving action, hire a guide and boat in Cahuita village. In addition to the usual Caribbean profusion of brightly colored coral and fish, there are two small shipwrecks in about 30 feet of water.

Even if you've never dove or snorkeled before, you really must rent some snorkeling gear and have a look at the easily accessible reefs. The undersea world of a tropical coral reef is simply too beautiful to miss (and it may not be around forever).

The forests are home to a splendid variety of animals, including howler and capuchin monkeys, sloths and the ubiquitous *pizotes*, as well as all sorts of aquatic and jungle birds. *Info:* There are two access points: Kelly Creek Ranger Station (Tel. 755-0461, open 6am-5pm) just south of the village of Cahuita; and Puerto Vargas Ranger Station (Tel. 755-0302, open 7am-4pm), 3 km further south. Entrance costs $6.

ONE TO TWO WEEKS ON THE SOUTH CARIBBEAN COAST

Hardcore beach bums and surfers would absolutely love a week or two in this laid-back region. More typical tourists, especially those with kids in tow, may start to get bored after a week, as the area doesn't have quite the wealth of touristy activities that you'll find around Manuel Antonio or Monteverde. If you want to seriously get into the tropical forest, then a week or two is almost mandatory, as the best wildlife refuges in the region are quite remote.

La Selva Biological Station
Operated by the Organization for Tropical Studies, south of Puerto Viejo, La Selva is a reserve covering almost 3,900 acres (1,600 hectares) set aside for research. The research station allows a few visitors, who can share comfortable but rustic room and

board while keeping an eye out for a tinamou, roseate spoonbill, curassow, band-tailed barbthroat or one of numerous LBBs (Little Brown Birds). Bring a raincoat, because the area averages well over a foot of rain per month. More than 240 scientific papers are published annually from research conducted at La Selva. *Info:* www.ots.duke.edu/en/laselva. Tel. 716-6987. $140 per day, double.

If you are seriously interested in tropical ecology, or would just like to have a close-up look at mountainous rain forest, then don't miss **Selva Bananito Lodge** (see *Best Sleeps*). The lodge is right at the edge of the largest protected area in all of Latin America: **Parque International La Amistad**, a vast and diverse biosphere with thousands of acres of undisturbed forest. Arrange transportation with the lodge, as they are somewhat remote. Naturalists and birders flock here to enjoy unspoiled, primary forest.

Gandoca-Manzanillo National Wildlife Refuge

This remote refuge near the Panamanian border sees few visitors. It features yet another spectacular beach, rain forests, mangrove swamps and a bit of coral reef. The lagoon is a nursery for tarpon, snook, dorado and tiny billfish. Local fishermen have secret tarpon fishing spots near the Panama border.

Leatherback sea turtles use this area for their nesting grounds, but there is no organized turtle worship as practiced in Tortuguero. If you encounter turtles involved in their nesting routine, you should keep 20 to 30 feet away and turn off all lights. Other aquatic animals include caimans, crocodiles, manatees and a rare species of dolphin called the *tucuxí*.

The beach here is absolutely magnificent, but the pounding surf makes it **unsafe for swimming**. *Info:* Gandoca, near the south end of the park, can be reached (at least in the dry season) by a tiny and terrible dirt road. There is said to be bus service. Manzanillo, on the coast in the middle of the park, has a few budget lodgings. You can also tour the park by boat from Cahuita.

7. NORTH-CENTRAL COSTA RICA

Northwest of San José lies a region of spectacular mountains, several of which are active volcanoes! Here the continental divide slopes down to the Pacific Ocean. You'll pass through many different ecosystems, from lush cloud forests to drier coastal forest.

The **Monteverde Cloud Forest Reserve** and the **Arenal volcano** are Costa Rica's most popular tourist destinations.

RECOMMENDED PLAN: Stay at one of the lodges around Santa Elena or Arenal, and make day trips to the volcano and one or more of the rain forest preserves in the area. If you're more interested in experiencing the cloud forest than in hanging around with crowds of other tourists, skip Monteverde and visit the Santa Elena Reserve instead.

ONE GREAT DAY IN NORTH-CENTRAL COSTA RICA

Due to distance and bad roads, it's not really practical to visit **Arenal** or **Monteverde** on a one-day trip from either San José or Nicoya, but if you are staying in one of the lodges near **Monteverde** or **Fortuna** (the town closest to Arenal), there are dozens of ways to spend a day. Seemingly hundreds of activities, represented by a similar number of glossy brochures, attract visitors.

If you have one day to spend in the area of **Arenal Volcano**, rise early to take advantage of any clearing in the cloud cover that might occur first thing in the morning. With luck you'll be able to enjoy breakfast at your lodge, with a view of the cone just past your cornflakes or *gallo pinto* (rice and beans, a typical Tico breakfast).

Arenal Observatory Lodge (see *Best Sleeps*) has a very nice view of the volcano from their dining room. The lodge is close to the volcano, with trails leading as close to the cone itself as you are allowed to go (not

Don't Miss...

• **Arenal Volcano** — This cone is one of the world's most photogenic and active volcanoes.
• **Tabacón Hot Springs** — Soak in the water amid lush greenery.
• **Santa Elena Reserve** — This wonderful wildlife reserve is far less crowded than more famous Monteverde.

Area Map of
**Arenal Volcano
&
Northern
Lowlands**

too close). Keep in mind that as Arenal is in the rain forest, it is usually obscured by clouds (that's where the rain comes from), so many visitors never actually get to see the cone. But the surrounding rain forest is worth the trip all by itself.

On a nice day, the volcano is observable from hundreds of vantage points, including from the streets of **Fortuna**. The nicer places to stay are lodges well outside Fortuna, closer to the cone. Fortuna is a smallish, bustling town with one purpose: booking and managing tourist activities in the area. It's not a particularly great place to hang out.

Best Views of the Lava Show

For several years the best view of the fiery action was looking at the volcano from the west, which made Arenal Observatory Lodge one of the best viewing points. Recently the lava flow has shifted to the other side of the cone, making the lodges **closer to Fortuna** more likely to have a good view.

After breakfast, catch a ride at your hotel for a walk through the forest around the volcano guided by a trained volcanologist. It will probably rain. Some lodges supply rubber boots and even ponchos. I suggest you bring your own plain, cheap rubber boots. You can buy them at a local hardware store for about $10. You'll certainly hear the mountain rumbling, and you might catch a glimpse through the trees of boulders tumbling down the slopes.

All the tourists love pricey **Tabacón Hot Springs**, so after lunch explore the spectacular pools and waterfalls amid lush green vegetation, as toucans and macaws fly overhead. There's also a major spa here, offering a variety of treatments, hot stone therapies, massages and yoga lessons. The springs and the nearby Tabacón Lodge are rumored to have been built directly on top of the lava flow from the last major eruption, now covered with jungle foliage. When the volcano blows again, the pyroclastic flow is scheduled to come right through the valley where these two lovely tourist attractions have been built. In other words: you could be toast.

Their already high prices climb steadily. As so often happens with popularity, quality suffers. I have recently been hearing complaints about high prices, poor food and inconsiderate service. On my visits, I found it to be overcrowded and overpriced.

However, Tabacón seems to be on every tourist's hot list, and the waterfalls and landscaping are quite impressive, so don't let me stop you. *Info:* Balneario Tabacón is open 11am-10pm; full day $45 adults, $25 kids (4-9). They also offer package deals including lunch or dinner. Some hotels offer discounted tickets for guests. www.costaricahotsprings.com. Information on the lodge is at www.tabacon.com; Tel. 460-2020.

Tabacón is not the only hot spring in the area. **Baldi Hot Springs** may not be quite as beautiful as Tabacón, lacking the picturesque waterfalls, but it does have 10 pools at different temperatures, a fully-equipped spa, a restaurant and a couple of swim-up bars. The vegetation is similarly lush, and there's a view of the Arenal cone.

The prices are lower and the crowds much smaller. Another bonus is that Baldi is located outside of the official Risk Zones, so you can swim in peace, without the fear of being incinerated. *Info:* Baldi Hot Springs is open 10am-10pm. Entrance is $25, or $40 including lunch or dinner. Children five and under half-price. www.arenal.net/baldi-hot-springs.htm; Tel. 282-8700.

After an afternoon soaking, hiking, or both, I suggest a quiet dinner at your lodge while enjoying a view of the volcano. Arenal can put on quite a fiery show at night if the sky is clear. Sometimes, even when things are overcast, you can see an ominous glow in the sky.

With only one day in the **Monteverde** and **Santa Elena** area, we'll have to

ALTERNATIVE PLAN: In the afternoon, go on a **hike with a bird specialist guide.** Expect to see three-wattled bellbirds, fasciated tiger herons, sunbitterns, laughing falcons, red-lored parrots, great curassows, northern jacanas, steely-vented hummingbirds, and of course keel-billed toucans. You could still go for a soak in the hot springs before dinner.

hustle a little to get it all done. Skip breakfast at tourist-packed **Stella's Bakery** and have great coffee and organic pastries at **Dulce Marzo Bakery and Café** on the main road a little bit closer to Santa Elena. Get a couple of cookies to take with you for later.

We now take the bold step of skipping the world-famous Monteverde Cloud Forest Preserve (known as the "crowd forest" to locals) and go past Santa Elena to the nicer and far less touristed **Santa Elena Cloud Forest Reserve**, where our guide will point out the elusive resplendent quetzal, three-wattled bell bird, and the occasional tinamou. Downtown **Santa Elena** offers a decent place to eat or two, and I suggest the **Treehouse** (see *Best Eats*) for a burger or pizza with an icy beer or two. But take it easy on the desserts because after lunch we're going zipping!

After a light meal, it's adrenaline time. All the tourists love **zip lines** and so-called **canopy tours**. **Sky Trek** is conveniently located near Santa Elena Cloud Forest Reserve. It is a huge operation with zip lines (wheeeeee!) through the forest, elevated walkways through the forest, and regular old paths through the forest. A lot of people are in and out of this place, and many of them spend part of their time screaming, so you can't expect to

see very many animals in the canopy posing for pictures. This is about fun, not nature. You can probably do something similar in Gatlinburg or Orlando but Costa Rica is famous for zip lines (oops, I mean canopy tours) so go for it. *Info:* www.skytrek.com. Tel. 645-5238. $45.

After excitement and stimulation, educational pursuits can fill the remaining part of the day. Numerous attractions line the strip between Santa Elena and Monteverde, and some of them are worth an hour or so of your time. It is easy to stop in at a serpentarium (snakes), ranarium (frogs), bat jungle, orchid garden, or art gallery.

Just outside the entrance to Monteverde Cloud Forest Preserve is the **Hummingbird Gallery**, a small souvenir shop with dozens of hummingbird feeders in their garden and therefore hundreds of hummingbirds flitting about. It's worth a visit just to watch the aerial daredevils go through their acrobatics. This is a *must do* for photographers. A very challenging subject, hummingbirds casually pose for tourists here and you are bound to get a few good shots. Turn on your motor drive and "spray and pray."

Just east of Santa Elena is a small botanical garden called **Orquídeas de Monteverde** (Monteverde Orchid Garden, Tel. 645-5510). This is a must-see for flower fanatics. Costa Rica is one of the top suppliers of orchids in the world, and the cloud forest habitat is where the most exotic varieties are found. Some of them are quite small, but all are beautiful. Entry $5.

The Garden restaurant at **Monteverde Lodge** (see *Best Eats*) will have the best meal in town. Their wine list is good, and their food is better than most of the tourist-filled places in the area. It's expensive, so if you have a bunch of kids or teenagers with you, go to one of the pizza joints instead. They probably wouldn't like the *ceviche* anyway. Nightlife is unremarkable in Monteverde, and you are probably tired after hiking all day anyway, so go back to your lodge and go to bed.

On the other hand, a **nighttime hike** can be a fascinating experience. After dark the creepy-crawly things come out and expose themselves for tourists to view. Most of the lodges can arrange for you to get into the cloud forest at night. If you can find an entomologist (bug person) guide, so much the better.

A FANTASTIC WEEKEND IN NORTH-CENTRAL COSTA RICA

With a weekend to spend in this region, you can easily visit both **Arenal** and **Monteverde** (or the less crowded **cloud forest preserve of Santa Elena**). You could also get in some windsurfing or kiteboarding on **Lake Arenal**, and spend some time hanging around the fun **town of Santa Elena**.

Arenal

Arenal is one of the world's most active volcanoes, and its conical shape is just what you'd expect. It spouts forth lava, smoke and noxious gases on a regular basis, and can be heard for miles around, sounding like a jet plane.

At night it's just like the fireworks in Sydney harbor. Bright red lava spews down the sides of the cone while glowing, freight-car-size globs of burning, noxious, lava guts disgorge into the air like Roman candles.

Getting to see the fun during the day is a rare treat, as the summit is almost always covered by clouds. Early in the morning is your best bet.

Arenal is a *stratovolcano*, which means one that has built up in layers over the years, each eruption adding a new layer of ashes and lava. It's part of the so-called "Ring of Fire," a chain of volcanoes that surround the coasts of the Pacific Ocean, where adjoining tectonic plates have crashed together, releasing the molten magma from deep beneath the Earth's surface.

The last major eruption (meaning one that forced the local people to evacuate) happened in 2000. Another big one occurred in 1968. Minor eruptions and spewage happen all the time, with an occasional bit of *pyroclastic flow* — this means an avalanche of rocks and boulders that can move at up to 50 miles per hour and (according to the US Geological Survey) "will destroy nearly everything in its path." You don't want to be in the area if this starts happening. See http://volcanoes.usgs.gov for lots more information on volcanoes.

The park features a number of trails from which you can see various types of volcanic action, as well as fields of lava and other evidence of past eruptions. The volcano itself isn't the only attraction: the cloud forest that covers the slopes has the usual variety of wildlife, and you can swim in a crystal-clear waterfall, surrounded by tropical greenery. *Info:* **Arenal Volcano National Park.** Tel. 461-8499. Open 8am-4pm. Entrance fee $7.

Arenal.net (www.arenal.net; Tel. 645-7070) runs a variety of tours in the Arenal region, including trips to the volcano, rafting and zip line canopy tours. Their website has lots of information about the volcano, including some astounding photos of eruptions. For a truly special perspective, take their horseback trip over the wonderful **Caño Negro Trail** from Arenal to Monteverde. You'll climb through the cloud forest, over the 4,500-foot Continental Divide, with spectacular views of the volcano and the lake ($65 per person, including pickup from your hotel and a light lunch).

Windsurfing & Kiteboarding
Lake Arenal is one of the world's top spots for windsurfing, thanks to a constant wind that averages 20 mph during the peak season (November through January). Any time during this period, you'll see radical windsurfers (and even gnarlier youngsters enjoying the latest extreme sport, kiteboarding) getting major air. Most of this action takes place on the west end of the lake past Nuevo Arenal. *Info:* Rentals and lessons are available at **Tilawa Windsurf Center** (www.windsurfcostarica.com; Tel. 695-5050). Rentals are also available at **Tico Wind Surf Center** (www.ticowind.com).

Monteverde
Monteverde always seems to be overflowing with fanny pack-wearing Gringos and their sticky kids wearing mouse ears. The **Monteverde Cloud Forest Preserve** is the most popular park in the country and, although it is quite large, the parts of it open to the public are usually busy, with only rare moments of privacy. On the other hand, the vegetation is spectacular, and the reserve is one of the few places you can see the flamboyant bird called the quetzal.

The drive to Monteverde is one of tourism's most famous **bone-jarring rides**. High in the mountains, there are only three winding, looping routes into Monteverde and all are only partially paved. Although the actual amount of driving that has to be done

on the unpaved portion is only about 20 miles, it is an especially bumpy, bouncy, rattling trip. The road surface is composed of millions of baseball- and softball-sized rocks.

The problem is not so much the mud as it is the rocks. It is impossible to go more than a couple of miles an hour, and you still come out of the trip with your head buzzing. Large buses, trucks, motorcycles and other local traffic ignore this dilemma and seem to pass at speeds more appropriate for Interstate highways. In the dry season, clouds of dust can be oppressive. It's about a three or four hour trip from San José, and three hours or so from Arenal around the lake.

There are 13 km of paths open to day hikers. **Guided walks** with local nature guides are available. You can take a morning or a night walk for about $15 per person. Advance reservations are wise. When it gets crowded, they close the paths, and you'll have to wait until someone else comes out before you can go in. Reserving a guided tour will eliminate that possibility. There's a visitors' center with a small restaurant and gift shop.

If you don't like crowds, head to less overrun parks like **Santa Elena Cloud Forest Reserve** or **Rincón de la Vieja** (see below) to enjoy the rain forests and wildlife in relative peace and quiet. The restaurants and lodges in this area can seem impersonal compared to other parts of the country that see fewer visitors. *Info:* **Monteverde Cloud Forest Preserve**. www.cct.or.cr. Tel. 645-5122. Visitors' center open daily 7am-4pm. Entrance fee: $13 adults; $6 kids (6-12); under six free.

To enjoy the cloud forests and flavor of the area without the crowds and tourist trappings, visit **Ecolodge San Luis**. This tropical biology research station, run by the University of Georgia, welcomes visitors, and has a few cabinas and bungalows available for overnight stays. If you're seriously interested in tropical ecology, this is a must (see *Best Sleeps*). It is located a little downhill from Monteverde in its own cloudy valley, yet convenient to town in case you feel the need for more prosaic tourist activities. I love the place and always seem to leave with good friends I didn't have before.

Hold the Cheese

The **cheese factory** is one of those "attractions" that everybody talks about, and it has some slight historical relevance (cheese making is the traditional industry of the Quakers who founded the town of Monteverde in the 1950s), but there is nothing of interest here except some (good) cheese for sale.

Santa Elena is a crowded but pleasant little tourist town with lots of bars, restaurants, tourist shops, art galleries, discos and lodging places along the strip that runs between the town and the park. The road is a spectacularly rutted mud and gravel affair that goes about three miles from the park to town. The strip is rapidly becoming clogged shoulder-to-shoulder with tourist "attractions" and will probably soon resemble some of the more notorious tourist areas in the US, like Orlando or Gatlinburg. Some of the animal-oriented attractions are quite worthwhile, especially the **Ranarium**, near Monteverde Lodge.

Santa Elena Cloud Forest Reserve
Santa Elena is far smaller than adjacent Monteverde (310 hectares versus 10,000), and sees far fewer visitors. This makes it much the better choice for a visit. The sights, and the facilities, are similar, and the tourist hordes don't seem to have discovered it yet.

There are four trails, with a total length of 12 km. The South Youth Challenge Trail leads to an observation tower and a couple of scenic overlooks. Santa Elena also has views of the Arenal volcano. The spectacular **Caño Negro Trail** climbs over the mountains, passing through several different ecosystems along the way and affording views of the volcano and the lake.

As at Monteverde, the visitors' center has a small café and a gift shop, and **guided walks** are available (two daily and one at night, about $15 per person). You can easily enjoy the park in just a couple of hours or spend an entire morning or afternoon.

The last time I was at Santa Elena, a half-tame peccary was wandering around the entrance to the park posing for pictures. I hadn't taken 10 steps down the trail when my guide softly said,

What is a Cloud Forest?

In northwestern Costa Rica, the high mountains of the continental divide are not far from the coast. As moisture-filled warm air blows in from the Pacific Ocean, it meets the barrier of the mountains, and condenses to form clouds. Visitors see a forest mysteriously **shrouded in fog**.

The 100% humidity and over four meters of rain every year create an incredibly lush flora. Damp-loving **lichens** and **mosses** cover every square inch of available space. Trees are draped with epiphytes (plants that grow in trees, such as **bromeliads** and **orchids**), creating an entire ecosystem high in the forest canopy. Many species of animals spend their entire lives up here, and you won't see them from the ground.

Many of Costa Rica's parks feature platforms high up in the canopy, where visitors can try to get a glimpse of some of these tree-dwellers. Don't worry about clambering up a ladder a couple of hundred feet — visitors are usually raised and lowered by means of ropes and pulleys.

It's well worth a visit to one of these **canopy platforms** — from the ground you're getting only half the picture. The patient visitor may be rewarded by a sight of arboreal monkeys or sloths, but most of the time you'll simply see a lot of LBBs – little brown birds – and perhaps some interesting insects.

"there's a quetzal" and pointed to a nearby tree. The three-wattled bellbird was not much further along.

On a three-hour hike, I encountered only two other groups of hikers. The day before in Monteverde I was never out of sight or hearing of other groups of bird venerators. *Info:* **Santa Elena Cloud Forest Reserve**, open 7am-4pm. Adults: $9; students $5. www.reservasantaelena.org. Tel. 645-5390.

ONE TO TWO WEEKS IN NORTH-CENTRAL COSTA RICA

There are several large and remote parks in the northwest part of the country, far from the tourist hordes. Take your time in **Monteverde** and **Arenal**, follow the weekend plan for both of these great destinations, then go a little way off the beaten path to the parks below – you'll be rewarded with spectacular volcano action and wonderful wildlife.

Rincón de la Vieja National Park

This park incorporates nine volcanoes, the large and active **Rincón de la Vieja** (the crater is some 15 km wide), and several inactive ones, including **Santa Maria**, at 1,916 meters one of the highest peaks in the region.

Here, in a little-visited part of the country, are all sorts of otherworldly

volcanic landscapes, including a lake that's steaming hot and others that are ice cold. There are puddles of boiling mud, and vents that spew sulfur dioxide and acid clouds (what fun!). There are sulfurous hot springs you can bathe in, and others that you definitely don't want to bathe in, or even walk too close to.

One of the most popular spots is the **Blue Lagoon**, a 30-minute hike from park headquarters. This exquisite swimming lake has a waterfall and a hot spring. Minerals in the rocks make the lake bright blue.

There are well-marked trails throughout the park. However, for safety's sake, and to learn about the unique ecology of the region, it's best to visit with a guide, which you can organize through any of the lodges in the region.

All sorts of wildlife are abundant. You may see a peccary, wild goat, tayra (a sleek weasel-like carnivore) or collared anteater, as well as three species of monkeys. If you're lucky, you might even see a pussycat. You'll certainly see some of the over 350 species of birds and beautiful **morpho butterflies**. The trees and vines are dense with epiphytes, including the national flower, the **purple orchid**.

This park is also a capital place for horseback riding and mountain biking. You can easily rent bikes, or arrange for horseback trips, in Liberia.

The jabbering tourist crowds haven't discovered Rincón de la Vieja. The area's lodges are comfortable and not yet crowded. I suggest cutting short your stay in Monteverde and spending at least two nights exploring the forests around the cones. *Info:* There are two ranger stations: **Santa Maria**, Northeast of Liberia; and **Las Pailas**, near Curubandé. Both are open 8am-4pm daily, and can arrange guided tours. Camping is available. Admission is $6.

Caño Negro National Wildlife Refuge

Caño Negro National Wildlife Refuge is a vast area of wetlands, which becomes a lake during the rainy season. It's a paradise for **waterfowl**, including various species of ducks, cormorants, anhingas, roseate spoonbills, ibis and jabiru storks (and you're sure to see crocodiles and caimans, which keep the birdies in check). The forests and grasslands are home to cougars, jaguars, ocelots, tapirs, peccaries and three species of monkeys.

There are no public facilities: you can visit only by boat. Most visitors come on organized tours, but guides and boats can be hired on the spot. The park supports tarpon and snook fishing in the rivers and lagoons. *Info:* There is a ranger station in the village of **Caño Negro**. Tel. 471-1309. Open 8am to 4 pm. $4 entry fee.

Guanacaste National Park

Guanacaste National Park was created in 1989 as a corridor between Santa Rosa National Park and the Orosí and Cacao volcanoes, allowing birds and mammals to migrate between coastal and cloud forest habitats. You can emulate the pumas, ocelots, peccaries, capuchin monkeys, howlers and coatis, and hike a trail that passes through several elevations and many different ecosystems. From some of the high lookout points, you can see the Lake of Nicaragua to the north and the Pacific Ocean to the west.

The Cacao Sector has precipitous trails to the summit of the **Cacao Volcano**. The Maritza Sector includes the continental divide, and the headwaters of several rivers, as well as dozens of ancient petroglyphs strewn through the jungle. The most remote area of the park is the Pitilla Sector, which has hiking trails to the **Orosí Volcano**. *Info:* There are three biological research stations in the park: **Cacao**, **Maritza** and **Pitilla**. All are near Potrerillos, which is about 20 miles north of Liberia on the Interamerican highway. All are open to visitors 8am-4pm, and have basic dormitory-style lodging available for tour groups.

8. THE NORTH PACIFIC COAST

With a somewhat drier climate than other parts of the country, the northern Pacific coast is a favorite destination year-round. The **Nicoya Peninsula** has dozens of tiny isolated beach towns, each with a spectacular strand, but each with its own unique character. This is the place to find your perfect personal beach.

RECOMMENDED PLAN: Fly into Liberia, and
one of the nearby beachfront resorts, where you ca
the full range of coastal activities, and make day trips to
interior. Avid anglers should head for Playa Flamingo, while
wildlife enthusiasts should check out Santa Rosa National Park
and the Cabo Blanco and Curú Wildlife Refuges. If time permits,
spend a day driving up and down the coast, exploring some of the
isolated little beaches.

ONE GREAT DAY ON THE NORTH PACIFIC COAST

The newish **international airport** near Liberia has become
quite active, with over 15 planeloads of North American
tourists a day flying in. It may be a good alternative to flying
to San José. Many visitors base themselves in the **beach
resort areas** within an hour or two drive of the airport, and
indulge in day trips to nearby attractions.

The town of **Liberia** has a rich colonial history and some
pretty old buildings, but the modern town is fairly unattrac-
tive, and has little more to offer than some US fast-food
restaurants and a couple of very run-down motels (al-
though there are several good ones an hour or so away) – so
below are some suggestions for spending one great day.

Most visitors to this region head for the **Nicoya Peninsula**, a
remote and sparsely populated area at the northwest corner of
the country. The coast is dotted with tiny towns and spectacular
beaches with mountains in the background. Nicoya sees a lot of
tourists, but there's a lot of space for them to spread out in, so the
region still has a laid-back, off-the-beaten-path atmosphere.
However, it's slowly but steadily being transformed by real
estate developments and new upscale resorts.

There are several ways to get to Nicoya. You can take a car ferry
from Puntarenas to Paquera or Playa Naranjo, which is conve-

Don't Miss...

- **Deserted beaches of the Nicoya Peninsula** — Each has its own flavor, so find the one that suits your personality.
- **Fishing at Playa Flamingo** — This is one of the country's top sport-fishing ports.
- **Cabo Blanco Reserve** — Enjoy the forest, the beach and the wildlife, minus the crowds of tourists.

nient if you're heading for Tambor or Montezuma at the south end of the peninsula. The small ferries sail on a first-come-first-served basis, and departure times can be unpredictable, so you need to arrive two hours early to be sure of getting on. If you're heading for the north of the peninsula (Samara or Tamarindo), going via the new Tempisque Bridge to the north is probably quicker. Another good option, if you're staying at one of the all-inclusive resorts, is simply to fly to one of the small airstrips along the coast, bypassing the roads, which can be dodgy in the rainy season. *Info:* **Naviera Tambor** (Tel. 661-2084) and **Ferry Peninsular** (Tel. 641-0515) run ferries to Paquera. **Coonatramar** (www.coonatramar.com; Tel. 661-1069) operates the one to Playa Naranjo.

The luxury beachfront hotel at **Punta Islita** would be an excellent choice for a base in the area. Another option, more moderately priced, is **Villa Alegre** (see *Best Sleeps*). You can spend much of your time lounging on the beach, and make day trips to go fishing, diving or to visit one of the wilderness preserves.

Many of the beach resorts offer all-inclusive packages, with lodging, food, and drinks all included in the price. This is a good option around here, as the most idyllic little beach towns have limited dining options outside the lodges. Of course, most lodges will gladly arrange tours for you as well.

There's quite a nice little website with a lot of useful information about the Nicoya region, and plenty of pictures, at www.nicoyapeninsula.com.

Guaitíl

Guaitíl is one of the few really world-class craft centers in Costa Rica. The people of the village take advantage of local clay deposits to make a variety of pottery. Nice pots and other ceramic items feature themes from the mythology of the indigenous Chorotegas people, including stylized jaguars, toucans, and the Chorotegas Fire God, a sort of snake with feathers. You can watch native potters at work and, of course, buy their attractive designs and even have them shipped back to the US. Women run most of the potteries. *Info:* Guaitíl is easy enough to get to, about 12 km off the main highway, past the town of Santa Barbara. One of several shops you can visit is **Willy's Pottery** (www.artesaniaswillysguaitil.com; Tel. 681-1283).

Playa Flamingo

This is a beautiful white-sand beach on a large horseshoe-shaped bay. It's not much of a town: most of the action centers around some new real estate developments. However, there are a couple of nice resorts (see *Best Sleeps*), and the marina offers the most extensive deep-sea fishing opportunities in the region (see *Best Activities*).

The Edge offers scuba diving trips to the nearby Santa Catalina Island area, and **Yellow Fin Sport Fishing** is one of several outfits offering deep-sea fishing charters for sailfish. See www.costaricaexotic.com to book these and all kinds of other tours in the region.

Curú Wildlife Refuge

Curú National Wildlife Refuge and Hacienda is one of the smallest wildlife preserves in Costa Rica, but it has at least five different distinct ecosystems, including both moist and dry coastal forests and mangrove swamps. Curú is actually a privately-run venture which includes a farm dedicated to sustainable agriculture and several ongoing conservation projects.

The proprietors are working to reintroduce spider monkeys and scarlet macaws, formerly extinct in the Nicoya region. They also rehabilitate orphaned animals for eventual release into the wild. Beware the spider monkeys that lurk near the entrance—the naughty little beggars have been spoiled by too much contact with humans, and idly loll about, waiting for unsuspecting tourists to take advantage of.

There are 11 hiking trails of varying lengths and levels of difficulty, on which you may encounter forest dwellers such as three species of monkeys, peccaries, kinkajous, anteaters and coyotes. The preserve is also home to wild cats including ocelots, pumas, and margays, as well as over 230 species of birds. The beach is a nesting ground for several species of sea turtles, and the mangroves form an important habitat where many types of fish and other sea creatures spend part of their life cycles.

Curú's beach is perfect habitat not only for turtles, but for tourists as well, with a spectacular setting, nice white sand and calm water that's safe for swimming. *Info:* Open daily 7am-4pm. Entrance: $8. Horses are available for rent. Cheap lodging is available in some very basic cabins near the beach. www.curuwildliferefuge.com.

Great, Deserted Beaches!

The Nicoya Peninsula has mile after mile of great beaches. So many that, even with beaucoup beachgoers (both Tico and tourist) visiting the region, many beaches are all but deserted. A typical Nicoya beach wraps around a crescent-shaped bay, framed by towering rock formations and backed by lush tropical forest. Many have tiny towns of varying degrees of funkiness, each with its own character.

Do you want an upscale resort, or a seedy-but-friendly little spot? A bit of nightlife and action, or total seclusion? Calm azure waters for swimming, or a killer break for surfing? Somewhere on the Nicoya Peninsula you can find the perfect beach for you! The northern region has several luxurious resorts, with championship golf courses and private airstrips. The southern coast is where you'll find the back-to-nature set going native.

If you love cats (and who doesn't?), visit **Hacienda Matambu**, near Curú, where an organization called Profelis rehabilitates small wild cats such as margays, jaguarundis and ocelots, many of them once kept (illegally) as pets, for release into the wild. *Info:* Open Mon, Wed, Fri 11am-3:30pm; Tue, Thu, Sat 8am-3:30pm. Entrance and guided tour: $10. www.profelis.com.

Gulf of Nicoya Islands

The Gulf of Nicoya has a host of islands of various sizes. Some have just a tiny village or two, and some are uninhabited by humans. All are absolutely teeming with birds. There are guided boat tours to several of the islands, and the hardy can visit by kayak.

The most popular is **Tortuga Island** (actually a pair of islands), just offshore from Curú. You can easily book a day trip here from Puntarenas, but the islands are by no means overrun (yet). The beaches are exquisite, gently sloping white sand perfect for swimming and snorkeling, and there are no permanent inhabitants to disturb the animals and birds you'll see along the hiking trails.

At the mouth of the Gulf, **Guayabo** and the **Islas Negritos** are protected biological reserves. You can't go ashore, but avid birders can watch the action from a boat.

Chira, the largest island in the gulf, mostly consists of an enormous expanse of mangrove swamps and salt pans, frequented by flocks of wading birds and swarms of mosquitoes. A couple thousand locals cultivate oysters and gather salt. There are said to be a couple of budget lodgings on the island.

Venado, the second-largest island, also has a couple of very basic accommodations and lots of bird-filled mangroves. You can take a tour here from Jicaral.

Other uninhabitated or almost-uninhabited islands are **Isla Caballo**, which has some lovely beaches, and **Isla San Lucas**, a former penal colony with a very colorful history.

A FANTASTIC WEEKEND ON THE NORTH PACIFIC COAST

You can base yourself in one of the various **Nicoya beach resorts** and head up to the rain forest for a weekend, especially if you haven't explored the areas around Monteverde and Arenal. But hanging out on the beach for a relaxing weekend, or visiting nearby national parks or reserves, is a fantastic way to spend your weekend!

Playa del Coco

A short trip from San José, Playa del Coco (called El Coco on some maps) is a typical little beach town with a main street lined with restaurants and souvenir shops. There's good surfing in the area, and you can find charter boats for fishing and diving. The immediate area has lots of coral reefs, and the more adventurous can take trips to the Murciélago Islands to the north.

Although the town itself is a little on the grubby side, a short walk from the center will bring you to some **spectacularly beautiful beaches**, dotted with huge rocks and backdropped by lush mountains.

Nearby, the smaller towns of **Ocotal** to the south, and **Playa Hermosa** and **Playa Panamá** to the north are more secluded and laid-back, with equally lovely beaches. Farther south are **Brasilito** and **Playa Flamingo**.

Alternatively, if you're inclined to get off the beach for a bit, head to either the little-visited **Cabo Blanco Reserve** or **Santa Rosa National Park** (see one-week plan for details). You will not be disappointed!

ONE TO TWO WEEKS ON THE NORTH PACIFIC COAST

A week or two in northwestern Costa Rica should give you plenty of time to spend a day **fishing** and a day or two **exploring the rain forests**, without taking too much time away from strenuous activities such as **lying around on the beach drinking rum**. You could divide your time between a couple of different beach resorts, but it probably makes more sense to pick the one that sounds right for you, and sleep there the whole week. However, be sure to spend a day or two driving along the coast, looking in at the various funky little beaches.

There are many little beach towns, and each has its own character. None of the towns in the Nicoya area is what you could call a major resort, but some are smaller and more laid-back than others. Some beaches are filled with Ticos out for a day's partying at the beach, some are the sites of all-inclusive luxury resorts, some cater to the surfer set, and yet others are the haunts of old hippies going to seed.

Playa Potrero

This is **one of the best beaches for swimming**, with very nice sand and mellow surf. Drive north via a bone-jarring dirt road to reach two isolated and beautiful spots, Playa La Penca and Playa Pan de Azúcar.

Playa Brasilito

This funky little beach town has a few budget lodgings and an especially nice swimming beach, with a nice expanse of sand.

Playa Conchal

As the name implies, this beach, at the village of Puerto Viejo near Brasilito, is **famous for seashells**. The beach is large, beautiful and never crowded, but strong currents make it dangerous for swimming.

This is where the prestigious all-inclusive **Paradisus Playa Conchal** is located, dominating the shoreline in front of the nicest part of the beach (see *Best Sleeps*). Other than that, the village consists of little more than a few budget lodgings, but there are several boats offering fishing and diving charters. Divers love the abundance of rays and sharks. The same currents that make it dodgy for swimming make it a top surfing spot.

Playa Tamarindo

Tamarindo is the largest village on the coast, such as it is. There is a "downtown" lined with tourist shops, restaurants, funky beach bars and hotels. Back streets hide more of the same. There is a festering surfer colony, and quite a few expats either retired or just going to seed in the tropics. You still occasionally see a couple of pigs roaming around, but those days are numbered.

The beach seems to be always filled with surfers. The break is close in, so it's a good place to watch the experts.

There are some great places to stay, and several restaurants vie with each other for serving the most interesting Pacific Rim seafood fusions. Nightlife is young and laid-back. Ironically, occasional dragnets through the kitchens of local restaurants by immigration authorities yield a few young Gringos working for bananas. They get shipped back home at Daddy's expense. *Info:* www.tamarindobeach.org.

No Lifeguard on Duty

Many of the beaches on the Pacific coast feature thunderous surf and wildly picturesque rock formations. While the surfing may be spectacular, swimming can be risky. At certain beaches, swimming is simply not safe. At most others, you need to use caution. If swimming rather than surfing is your goal, look for someplace in a protected bay. Always check local conditions, stay close to shore, and be extremely cautious at isolated beaches far from towns.

Playa Junquillal

This tiny town has a large secluded beach. South of here, the beaches are stunning and almost deserted. **Samara** is a nice beach, popular with Ticos.

Once past **Carrillo**, roads are interesting to say the least, with some dodgy river crossings. At some of these fords, you won't find your way safely across without local help, so be patient and seek detailed directions from the locals when you see them wading across.

Playa Ostional

Ostional is famous for the vast hordes of **Ridley turtles** that pull in from July to November when they come to lay eggs. Even though the beach is 8 km long the turtles insist on using only a small stretch of less than 1 km, and rarely lay eggs anywhere else. They prefer the last quarter of the moon to do their thing.

Playa Islita

Dominated by Punta Islita Lodge (see *Best Sleeps*), the beach is long and curving with rocky points at each end. Tourists race up and down on **horses**, and the medium-size surf is popular with boogie boarders and beginning surfers. The hotel has a great pool and bar near the sand.

Tambor

Down here towards the southern end of the peninsula, the atmosphere is more laid-back, with **surfers and nature lovers** staying in budget lodgings, in contrast to the luxury resorts and big-buck fishing operations of the north. Tambor is a quiet little

town with a beautiful beach, quite good for swimming, and a few sleazy, colorful beach bars where locals and expats swap travel stories.

Montezuma

This secluded village, at the end of a long and steep road, is famous around the world for its **hippie vibe**. Rastas, New Agers and hairy backpackers mingle in the town center. Vegetarian fare and lively bars are easy to find. The town is surrounded by especially lush forest, and has a nice beach and various picturesque waterfalls nearby. Fishing, diving and horseback riding tours are on offer.

Cabo Blanco Reserve

At the southern tip of the peninsula, this very wild and remote wilderness reserve is **one of Costa Rica's finest parks**. It has the distinction of being the first protected area in the country, established in 1963 thanks to the efforts of Swedish environmentalist Nicolas Wessberg, but it was only recently opened for public visits.

The well-marked **Sueco Trail** is 4.5 km of ups and downs through luxuriant forest, finally leading to the beach, where you'll see the white (with seabird guano) cape that gives the park its name. The climate here is drier than in the uplands around Monteverde, with many evergreen trees. You'll see a vast variety of **seabirds**, and if you're patient, you may see white-tailed deer, anteaters, three kinds of monkeys, peccaries, coyotes, and maybe even signs of an ocelot. *Info:* The ranger station is two miles south of Cabuya (past Montezuma), on a poor road that may be impassable during the rainy season. The park is open Wed-Sun 8am-4pm. Admission is $8. You can get a taxi to the reserve, and also arrange for guided tours, in Montezuma. The website at www.caboblancopark.com has a bit of info on local tour operators and rental homes.

Mal País

If Montezuma is a hippie hangout, this is definitely a **surfer town**. There's nothing here but a very cheap surfer lodging called Mal País Surf Camp and Resort (www.malpaissurfcamp.com), a few lodges, a couple of bars and the totally awesome break.

Santa Rosa National Park

Here at the northwestern corner of Costa Rica, the Nicaraguan border traverses a narrow strip of land between the Pacific Ocean and Lake Nicaragua. The region was destined by geography to be the site of several historic happenings.

Santa Rosa National Park was established in 1971 to commemorate the site of the Battle of Santa Rosa, an 1856 battle in which Costa Rica fought off an invasion attempt by Nicaraguan troops allied to American adventurer William Walker. During the battle, a young man from Alajuela named **Juan Santamaría** became one of Costa Rica's national heroes when he bravely set fire to the Nicaraguans' stronghold, getting killed in the process.

Nicaraguan dictator Somoza made an abortive attack here in 1955. In the 1980s the CIA had a secret airstrip and a training camp for the Nicaraguan contras in what is now the Murciélago Sector of the park.

This large (495 square km) coastal park is part of a network of parks in the region, called the Guanacaste Conservation Area. Santa Rosa contains at least **a dozen different habitats**, including deciduous forest, marshlands, and mangrove swamps, as well as open scrub-dotted savannas, a legacy of former slash-and-burn agriculture.

Santa Rosa is an excellent place to observe wildlife, especially in the dry season, when animals come to drink at the few watering holes, and the comparatively open terrain makes the critters a little easier to spot. The park boasts 115 mammal species and 250 bird species. You're sure to spot coatis, deer and a monkey or two (howler, spider, and capuchin varieties). Coyotes, tapirs and peccaries are a bit more elusive. If you're really lucky, you may see a wild cat: jaguars, pumas, ocelots, margays and jaguarundis all live in the park. The **best trails for spotting animals** are the short (1.5 km) **Naked Indian Trail** and the longer **Los Patos** and **Laguna Escondida trails**.

The park is easily accessible by road, with two ranger stations just off the Interamerican Highway. At the Santa Rosa Sector to the south you'll find Hacienda Santa Rosa (also known as La Casona), an old colonial plantation house where the famous battle of 1856 was fought. It's now a slightly interesting historical museum. Several hiking trails originate here.

Beaches in Santa Rosa

There are a couple of beautiful beaches in the park, which are very hard to get to, and therefore quite untouristed. **Playa Nancite** is one of a handful of nesting sites in the world for the endangered olive Ridley sea turtles, who visit from August through December. Humans wishing to visit must have a permit, which you can get from the ranger station.

Playa Naranjo and its Witches Rock are famous for quite a different reason. The long tubular break is a legend among surfers. There's a so-called road leading from Hacienda Santa Rosa to Nancite and Naranjo, but it's passable only with a 4WD vehicle, if at all.

There's another ranger station to the north, at the Murciélago Sector, about 15 km from the highway. The road is challenging, with several river crossings, but usually passable with a 4WD vehicle. It ends at **Playa Blanca**, an **unbelievably beautiful white-sand beach** frequented by *pizotes* and other local critters, but not by tourists. South of here are several equally beautiful and even more isolated beaches, accessible only by boat.

The Santa Elena Peninsula is one of the few areas on the Pacific coast with extensive **coral reefs**. The most famous dive site is the **Islas Murciélagos** (Bat Islands), which is frequented by the gentle giants of the sea, filter-feeding whale sharks, as well as several much less cuddly species of shark. Advanced divers only, please. There's nothing on the islands but a small ranger station with very minimal camping facilities.

You can hire a local *panga* at the little fishing village of Jobo to visit the Bat Islands or any of the isolated beaches, but for dive charters, you'll have to go to Playa Flamingo, on the Nicoya Peninsula to the south. *Info:* The main ranger station is at the Santa Rosa Sector (take Highway One 37 km north from Liberia, then take a dirt road about 6 km). There's a camping area with restrooms and showers. Open daily 8am-4pm. www.acguanacaste.ac.cr. Tel. 666-5051. Entrance fee $6.

The entrance to the Murciélagos Sector is 26 km further north from the entrance to Santa Rosa Sector, then 9 km down a dirt road. Open daily 8am-4pm. There's a camping area with restrooms and showers. There's also a very rustic camping area at Naranjo Beach. Always inquire about local road conditions, and keep your passport handy, as there are several police checkpoints in the area.

9. THE CENTRAL PACIFIC COAST

Between the Nicoya Peninsula to the north and the Osa Peninsula to the south are some of Costa Rica's most frequented beach areas, including the country's two largest resort areas: **Jacó** and **Manuel Antonio**. However, secluded strands are not hard to find.

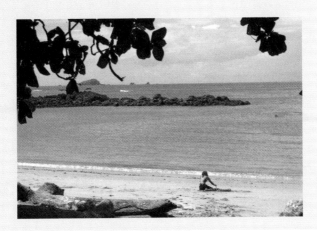

RECOMMENDED PLAN: If you'd like a lively beach town with lots of young people and a hopping nightlife scene, stay near Jacó. If you'd prefer a quieter, more upscale resort area, stay around Manuel Antonio. Both places have excellent beaches, and both provide easy access to the wildlife wonders of Manuel Antonio National Park and the world-class sport-fishing fleet in Quepos.

Coming down from San José, the road descends steeply to the palm-studded coast with spectacular views out over the Pacific. Shortly before reaching the coast, you'll cross a bridge over a river at **Tárcoles**. The river below is stiff with crocodiles! Even if you're just passing through, do stop and have a quick look. Park on the side, give a little kid a buck to watch your car, and join the parade of tourists observing the somnolent saurians.

Don't Miss...

- **Crocodiles in the river at Tárcoles** – They're hanging out for all to see.
- **Fishing off Quepos** – It's Costa Rica's largest sport-fishing center.
- **Manuel Antonio National Park** – It's worth braving the tourist hordes.

There's a gift shop just before the bridge and usually a few people selling water coconuts (*pipas*). Vendors will slice the tops off the coconuts for you with a machete. Poke in a straw and enjoy! They are quite refreshing. You can usually buy mangos, watermelons, papayas and pineapples here. Try some of each.

ONE GREAT DAY ON THE CENTRAL PACIFIC COAST

With just one day, your best bet is to either head for one of the great **beach towns** described later in this chapter, or visit **Carara National Park**, especially if you enjoy birdwatching. However, be aware that this park, easy to get to from the capital, gets very crowded.

Carara National Park

Near the coast, this park is easy to visit on a day trip from San José. The downside of its easy accessibility is predictable: it's almost always mobbed with tourists, including cruise ship passengers bused in for day trips. If you have more time to spare, skip this one.

Carara is **a favorite of birders**. Located in a transition zone between the Pacific rain forest ecosystem and the drier habitats to the north, the park has a particularly rich roster of bird species. The comparatively open woodland makes birds easier to spot than in the thick rain forest.

The park is thick with scarlet macaws, and you may also spot toucans, aracaris, tinamous, and all sorts of herons, anhingas, egrets and other water birds. You will certainly see many examples of the North American Twitcher, which may be almost as interesting to watch as the birdies. *Info:* The **Quebrada Bonita** ranger station and park headquarters is 2 miles south of the bridge over the Tárcoles River. There are two short hiking trails (each about 1 km). Buses from San José stop at the station. No lodging or camping is available in the park. Entrance fee is $8. Hours are 8am-4pm. Tel. 200-5023.

A FANTASTIC WEEKEND ON THE CENTRAL PACIFIC COAST

Jacó is a good choice to base yourself for a weekend, but it is popular, and that means lots of people. If you love the beach, but can't stand the crowds at Jacó, no problem! Between Jacó and **Quepos/Manuel Antonio** are a lot of pretty little beaches, mostly deserted. Some have cabinas to stay in, and little restaurants.

Playa Jacó

This is the biggest and most visited beach town in the country, popular with Ticos, tourists, beach bums, surfers and anglers, offering every kind of watery activity you could wish. It's within easy weekend-trip range of San José. This is the place to go if you want a lively beach town not too far off the beaten path.

The beach itself is great, fine for swimming, surfing, tanning or just sitting at a bar and watching the young ladies strutting about in their bikinis and the young men playing soccer.

There are several nice resorts in the immediate area, but the only one in town that's any good is the **Hotel Club Del Mar**, right on the beach (see *Best Sleeps*).

And speaking of hotels here: most stink. They're generally cheap and dirty, with surfers camping in the parking lot. The noisy strip through town is annoying, lined with t-shirt shops and seemingly hundreds of places hustling half-day tours to Monteverde (not practical) and overpriced fishing trips in leaky local *pangas*. Tacky bars heave with dubious ladies of the night and dreadlocked, grungy North Americans offer drugs. The tourist restaurants are overpriced. The beautiful beach is thronged with young, sexy surfers doing their thing like some sort of exotic seals. They won't bother you. You can avoid the noise and crap easily enough. You can sit in a bar and gaze out over all this while sipping a Bavaria Negra. Know what to avoid and the place can be lots of fun.

ONE TO TWO WEEKS ON THE CENTRAL PACIFIC COAST

With one or two weeks, you can explore some great beaches in this area and still venture further afield, hanging out in Quepos and visiting Manuel Antonio National Park, Dominical (only if you surf, otherwise give it a miss) and the other nearby national parks: Ballena and Chirripó.

Quepos

This is a typically grubby little port town, but it happens to be the **biggest sport-fishing center** in the country. If your goal is to catch a billfish, you'll have no problem finding a charter boat here. You can sleep, eat and party in one of the upscale places in Manuel Antonio, right next to Quepos. But don't miss **El Gran Escape** in Quepos for gigantic fish sandwiches, burgers and beer.

Manuel Antonio

This is not much of a town, but rather a strip leading from Quepos to the park, lined with hotels, restaurants, bars and tour operators.

Compared to Jacó, Manuel Antonio attracts an older, more affluent crowd. There are more big-buck hotels here than anywhere else in CR. There are a couple of wonderful beaches, great for swimming, but the hotels are *near* the beach, rather than right on the beach.

Manuel Antonio National Park

Established in 1972, Manuel Antonio is the smallest (1,624 hectares) but **most visited national park** in the country. The vast flocks of tourists are such that some days they admit no more visitors after late morning.

There's a variety of hiking trails, winding along the beaches and through the forest. Most are not very well marked. There are 109 species of mammals and 184 of birds in the park. Manuel Antonio is one of the best places to see sloths (the Spanish name is *perezoso*, which simply means "lazy"), both two- and three-toed.

Manuel Antonio is one of the few places where you're likely to see the tiny squirrel monkey (*mono tití*). You're also likely to see white-faced and howler monkeys, agoutis, *pizotes*, opossums and iguanas. The forests are home to lots of scarlet macaws and toucans, and the coast has vast flocks of sea birds, such as pelicans, frigate birds and anhingas.

The beaches in the park are beautiful and pristine, from **Espadilla** in the north, to **Manuel Antonio** beach, the best for swimming, to **Third Beach** with its tidal pools, to the secluded **Puerto Escondido** in the south. *Info:* Tel. 777-0654. Open Tue-Sun 7am-4pm. Entrance fee $7. www.manuelantoniopark.com is a privately-operated web site with links to various tour operators and lodging in the area.

Dominical

From Quepos south to Dominical, the road is particularly bad, passing through massive palm oil plantations. After that you'll meet up with the route coming down from San Isidro. The road from here on south was excellent a few years ago, when it was built. Alas, it hasn't been properly maintained, and now there are potholes that could swallow a whale shark.

Dominical is a **dirty and unpaved** town, with a lot of construction going on. It seems random and unplanned, with garbage piles next to restaurants, and trenches carrying septic wastes snaking through the village.

There's a **highly colorful surfer scene** going on. The beach at Dominical is great for surfing, but dangerous for swimming. The beaches to the south are super and only lightly touristed.

Restaurants include unclean places with terrible food and several blaring sports bars. I try not to eat in Dominical if possible, but there are a few places attempting tropical macrobiotic/Pac Rim/ Marin County/fusion things with organic mango sauce at high prices.

Ballena National Marine Park
South of Dominical is **Ballena National Marine Park**, which was created to protect the coral reefs and the humpback whales that congregate offshore from December through May (the name *ballena* means "whale"). Most of the park is underwater, but it includes a couple of stunningly beautiful beaches, Playas Ballena and Uvita, that are easily accessible from the coast road.

There are no park facilities to speak of, and little to see from shore other than the wonderful beaches. The beaches are excellent for strolling around on, especially at low tide when you can walk way out on the rocks. You can charter a boat from Dominical to snorkel the reefs, or hang out with the whales when they're around. *Info:* The ranger station is near Rancho La Merced Wildlife Refuge, just north of Ballena, and is open 8am-4pm.

Chirripó National Park
On the slopes of **Cerro Chirripó**, Costa Rica's highest mountain (12,530 feet), **Chirripó National Park** encompasses several different habitats within a difference in elevation of over 8,000 feet. Cloud and rain forest give way to sparse high-altitude landscape called *paramo*, or "wet desert."

Climbing all the way to the peak is not for the casual visitor. Although no technical mountain-climbing skills are required, it's a steep 30-mile round trip, with rain a virtual certainty, and temperatures that can be below freezing in winter. Most climbers make the trip over three days, stopping to camp at Valle de los Crestones (which has bunk beds, a cooking area, and cold showers), about halfway up. If you reach the top, you'll have a spectacular view of both oceans and Costa Rica's mountain backbone.

You don't have to make the three-day trek to the summit to enjoy Chirripó. Shorter hikes from **San Gerardo de Rivas**, the gateway to the park, are quite feasible.

The climate up here is exquisite. Tropical vegetation from mangos to coconuts is as lush as you please, but the air is pleasantly cool. *Info:* Take the Interamerican Highway to San Isidro de El General, then take a smaller road north to Rivas, then San Gerardo de Rivas. The ranger station in San Gerardo de Rivas is open for visitors 5am-12pm. Call 771-5116 in San Isidro de El General to make reservations at the Los Crestones base camp.

10. THE SOUTH PACIFIC COAST

The southwestern corner of Costa Rica is the most remote region of the country, and features some of her most pristine rain forests, fantastic fishing and spectacular surfing. This sparsely populated region was historically a major gold-mining area, but the major activities today are cattle ranching and ecotourism.

RECOMMENDED PLAN: Spend a few days at Corcovado Lodge Tent Camp, and explore the rain forest and the beach. If time permits, visit one of the lodges near Puerto Jiménez (Crocodile Bay or the Iguana Lodge), and enjoy some of the finest fishing in the world.

ALTERNATE PLAN: Fly down to Drake Bay and explore Corcovado National Park from the northern end. Take a dive trip to **Caño Island**. Take a **night walk in the rain forest** with Tracie the Bug Lady and see 10,000 spiders.

There are no sights in this region that really make sense for a one-day visit. If you only have a day to spare, you'll have a better time on the Nicoya Peninsula or one of the rain forest areas in the north of the country around Monteverde (see previous sections).

A FANTASTIC WEEKEND ON THE SOUTH PACIFIC COAST

The centerpiece of this region is the **Osa Peninsula**, the most remote and isolated area of the country. Much of the peninsula is occupied by the national park and a forest reserve. The entire area is thick with wildlife. Even outside the park's boundaries, you'll see lots of scarlet macaws and toucans. Monkeys are quite common, including the adorable little squirrel monkey (*mono tití*), which is found only here in the southern part of the country.

Thanks to several small airstrips, a weekend getaway to the Osa Peninsula is just feasible. Costa Rica Expeditions, which runs **Corcovado Lodge Tent Camp** (see *Best Sleeps*), offers a 3 day/2 night tour that could be the trip of a lifetime for any nature lover.

You'll take a one-hour flight from Pavas Airport to a tiny seaside landing strip at **Carate**. From here, you walk about 40 minutes along the beach to the lodge (a member of the lodge staff will meet you at the airfield and bring your luggage along in a donkey cart). There's time for an afternoon hike in the coastal rain forest. After a hearty dinner, washed down with lots of fresh fruit juice or a couple of beers at the bar, you'll go to sleep to the sounds of the surf and the jungle.

Don't Miss...

- **Corcovado National Park** — It's the most remote and unspoiled of Costa Rica's many parks.
- **Fishing** — The Golfo Dulce is thick with roosterfish, a resplendent and hard-fighting member of the jack family. Sailfish and marlin beckon offshore.
- **Wilson Botanical Garden** — The finest botanical garden in Central America is easy to visit on your way in or out of the area.

The next day, you'll take a guided tour through the forest, including a visit to a platform high up in a tree, where you can check out the **rain forest canopy**. Much of the wildlife of the forest lives high up in the trees, invisible from the ground. A few lodges have treetop platforms like this one. It's definitely worth going up to have a look, though it may not be quite as exciting as the guides make it out to be: most of what you'll see will be little brown birds.

After a second night at the peaceful tent camp (if you can't relax here, there's no hope for you), it's time to fly back to San José. Exactly when you go depends on the tide, as the only route back to the airstrip is along the beach. *Info:* 3 day/2 night tours from $508 per person, double occupancy (or $169 per person per day), including lodging, meals, guides, airfare and transfers. See www.costaricaexpeditions.com.

Best Birding

All of Costa Rica's parks and reserves are rich in bird species. To maximize the number of additions to your life list, visit several parks with different types of habitat (cloud forest, dry forest, coastal mangroves, etc.) The superlative destination is remote **Corcovado**, your best bet to see something really rare. Don't pass by **Carara National Park** — it's full of tourists, but its location between northern and southern climatic regions gives it a unique mix of species, and the relatively open landscape makes them easy to spot.

Would you rather spend your weekend wrestling with massive billfish than watching the monkeys? No problem! *Pura vida!* Take a plane to **Puerto Jiménez**, a short ride from **Crocodile Bay**, a modern, easily accessible lodge where you can enjoy some of the finest fishing in the world (see *Best Sleeps*).

Las Cruces Biological Station/Wilson Botanical Garden

Las Cruces, located up in the mountains near the border with Panama, is one of three biological stations run by the Organization for Tropical Studies. It incorporates the world-famous Wilson Botanical Garden, generally considered **the best in Central America**, with over 1,000 species of plants. Las Cruces is about a 5-hour drive from San José, but it would make an easy day trip if you're staying in the Golfito area.

Well-maintained (but somewhat hilly) trails amble through several types of habitat. You'll experience a wealth of bromeliads, heliconias, lilies, ferns, groves of bananas, and what many call the world's largest collection of palms. The area has over 230 species of birds, including tanagers, trogons, blue-headed parrots, falcons and a profusion of hummingbirds. Monkeys and sloths are plentiful.

For really serious rain forest explorers and researchers, Las Cruces is a base station for exploring the nearby **La Amistad Biosphere Reserve**, the vast (472,000 hectares) and remote park that encompasses the peaks of the Talamanca mountain range.

Area Map of
Osa Peninsula
&
Drake Bay

Nicaragua

Puntarenas

Panama

Dominical

Playa Uvita
Uvita
Piñuela

Playa Ballena
Parque Nacional
Marino Ballena

Puerto
Cortés
Rio Terraba
Palomar
Sur

Humedales
Nacional
TÈrraba -
Sierpe

Sierpe
Rio Sierpe

Puntarenas

KEY
Ferry Crossing

Surf Break

National Park

Forest Reserve

Drake
Bay
Reserva Forestal
Golfo Dulce
Rincon

P.N.
Piedras
Blancas

Golfito

Golfo

Parque Nacional
Corcovado

PENINSULA DE OSA

Dos
Brazos

Puerto
Jiménez
Zancudo

Playa Corcovado

Playa
Zancudo

Dulce

Reserva Forestal
Golfo Dulce

Carate
Agua Buena
Playa
Sombrero

Pavones

Playa
Madrigal
Playa Piro
Cabo Matapalo
Rio Clara

The lodge has 12 basic but very neat and clean cabins with private bath and nice balconies, that go for about $160 double, including all meals and one guided half-day walk. *Info:* Las Cruces is 5 km south of San Vito, just off the highway between San Vito and Ciudad Neily. Guided walks last 2-3 hours and cost $15-24 for adults and $8-12 for kids. Night walks and dawn bird walks are also happening. Reservations are recommended. www.esintro.co.cr. Tel. 524-0628.

ONE TO TWO WEEKS ON THE SOUTH PACIFIC COAST

If you have a week or more, you could easily enjoy both sea and forest, either by dividing your time between **Corcovado** and **Crocodile Bay**, or by staying at one of the other lodges in the area, such as the **Iguana Lodge** or the remote and luxurious **Lapa Ríos** (see *Best Sleeps*), and booking a fishing trip with one of several excellent captains out of Puerto Jiménez.

Most visitors fly in, but to get the full Osa Peninsula experience, **drive down from San José**. This is adventure travel, and not for those with limited time. Even the drive from the main highway to Puerto Jiménez takes half a day. It's probably best not to attempt it without four-wheel drive.

The road from the highway used to be paved for a few miles, but the potholes have now become so bad that it isn't any more drivable than the dusty washboard that follows. You'll bounce along past mile after mile of cattle ranches, wondering if there can possibly be a town out here. But the road just keeps going on, until you reach grubby little Puerto Jiménez, on the coast.

Getting around by car down here requires a sturdy vehicle and plenty of time. The tiny towns are sleepy, sun-baked and seedy. The few foreigners living in them answer to a similar description. Some are globetrotting young surfers, others are colorful characters who may be hiding from the IRS or more sinister agencies (listen to *The Gringo's Tale*, a song by Steve Earle that probably wasn't written about Costa Rica, but certainly sounds as if it could have been). Most visitors to this area stay at one of the excellent jungle lodges, several of which are easily accessible by air.

Puerto Jiménez

This run-down little town is of interest to tourists only as a place to **fly into and shop for supplies** on the way to one of several excellent wilderness lodges in the area. It does have a couple of decent low-priced restaurants.

From here, the road really gets interesting, as it winds along the coast around the peninsula to Carate, the end of the road, and almost to Corcovado. You'll have to cross several rivers, some by rickety bridges, some by driving right through the water. Be sure to ask the locals about current road conditions, and don't attempt it at all during the rainy season.

Casa de Orquídeas

Across the bay from Puerto Jiménez, and accessible only by boat, this **charming botanical garden** has tropical wonders such as a palm tree ten feet in diameter, a lipstick tree, all sorts of exotic fruits and spices, and the usual variety of orchids, bromeliads, and their attending butterflies and hummingbirds. Arrange a tour through your lodge, or catch a boat in Puerto Jiménez or Golfito.

Corcovado National Park

The park that is often called **the "crown jewel"** of Costa Rica's vast park system, and that *National Geographic* has called "the most biologically intense place on Earth," includes the **largest swath of primary forest on the Pacific coast of America**, and one of the few substantial areas of lowland tropical rain forest remaining in the world.

Remoter than Thou

Corcovado is often referred to as the remotest of Costa Rica's national parks, but it would be more accurate to say that it's the remotest of the parks that are reasonably accessible to visitors. The prize for the most remote and unexplored park must go to La Amistad International Park, an enormous area of 472,000 hectares that is connected to a similar park across the border in Panama.

Encompassing the highest peaks of the Talamanca mountain range, there are no villages in the park, nor even any roads to speak of. The closest outposts of civilization are two research stations operated by the Organization for Tropical Studies: La Selva on the northern border of the park, and Las Cruces near the southern edge.

Either can arrange a visit, but this is no place for a day hike with the kids. Only researchers and hard-core hikers willing to spend several days camping in the backwoods will witness the wonders of this unspoiled wilderness.

This large park (105,000 acres) varies in elevation from the coast to the 2,444-foot peak of Cerro Rincón. The area receives 120-240 inches of rain per year.

The area that is now the park used to be the preserve of gold miners and loggers, who caused a lot of devastation. In the 1970s the government placed restrictions on mining and logging, and established the national park, and the jungle has rapidly reclaimed the land.

This large, remote and comparatively untouristed park is arguably **the most likely place to see elusive critters** such as big cats (ocelot, margay, jaguar, puma), tapirs, river otters, peccaries and rare brocket deer, while familiar draws such as monkeys (all four species), *pizotes*, scarlet macaws, toucans and orchids are plentiful. Corcovado boasts 140 species of mammals, 120 species of reptiles and amphibians, and 375 species of birds.

Corcovado is not a destination for the casual visitor. Just getting here takes some time and some planning. Some of the trails are long and rugged, with river crossings and steep climbs.

Some sections may be closed during the rainy season. The heat, the insects and all the other hazards of the rain forest are at their most intense here (except the crowds).

There are well-maintained trails around and between the various ranger stations. You can take a short hike on a fairly flat trail along the coast, or a steep one up into the interior. The really hardy can hike from the park border all the way to Sirena (16 km from Madrigal, 23 km from San Pedrillo). You'll be wading across several rivers, and **snakes are abundant**, so the rangers strongly recommend rubber boots.

The **Sirena Biological Station** is the heart of Corcovado, paradise for twitchers and wildlife lovers. If you want to see the crocodile eat the baby anteater, this is the place to come. *Info:* Most tourists come to Corcovado National Park on package tours,

The Bug Lady

Tracie Stice (the Bug Lady), offers the best tour I have taken in Costa Rica. Biologist Tracie and her spotter, Carlos, are based in Drake Bay near Corcovado, and take small groups into the forest at night with flashlights and night vision goggles to see nightlife, focusing primarily on, well, bugs.

She is a biologist who has lived in the area for many years and knows more about insects than seems possible. She describes the exotic sex lives of the tiny critters, and makes it all somehow much more interesting than my high school biology teacher did. She promises to show you thousands of spiders. And she delivers. Her spotter, Carlos, walks ahead of the group looking for the unusual and fascinating, leaving Tracie time to explain and tell stories about who gets to eat who instead of smoking a cigarette after the insect sex act. Her tour is worth a trip to Drake Bay all by itself. *Info:* www.thenighttour.com. Tel. 382-1619.

but you're welcome to visit on your own. There are three ranger stations at the borders of the park: **San Pedrillo** in the northwest, **La Leona** in the southeast, and **Los Patos** in the northeast. Park headquarters is at **Sirena**, deep in the heart of the park, and accessible only by foot, plane or boat (advance reservations are required). You can camp at any of the stations. Very basic lodging and meals are available at Sirena. The entrance fee is $8. www.corcovado.org. Tel. 735-5036, 735-5580.

Drake Bay

An alternate jumping-off point for Corcovado National Park is **Drake Bay**, on the northern side of the park. This is a *very* remote spot. There is a road connection that's supposedly passable with a 4x4 during the dry season, but most visitors arrive by plane or boat. Drake Bay is an area rather than a town. There's a small village called Agujitas, and a bunch of jungle lodges spread out around the large and picturesque crescent-shaped, crocodile-infested bay. A couple of operators offer dive and sightseeing trips to nearby Caño Island.

Caño Island

This small island, 20 kilometers offshore and visible from Drake Bay, is an **uninhabited biological reserve**. The forest is beautiful, but no more interesting than that of nearby Corcovado. However, an excursion to the island is a good excuse to take a boat ride and see the whales and dolphins. The island boasts some coral, and is an excellent spot for diving. Snorkeling is good when the waves are calm.

Isla Cocos (Cocos Island)

The **world's largest uninhabited island** lies about 480 kilometers to the southwest of the Costa Rican mainland. The entire island is a national park. Although it has a number of birds that are found nowhere else in the world, as well as lush forest with many picturesque waterfalls, the island itself is visited almost exclusively by biological researchers. Numerous expeditions in search of pirate treasure have dug enormous holes around the island. Serious divers visit the nearby waters on liveaboard dive boats to swim with the huge schools of **scalloped hammerhead sharks**, manta rays and other large pelagic species (see *Best Activities*).

On the eastern side of the **Golfo Dulce**, across the bay from the Osa Peninsula, are a couple of small villages with some lodges and fishing resorts.

Best Surfing

The very hippest surf spot of them all is **Pavones**, where the quarter-mile-long left break comes close enough to shore that you can toss a beer to passing surfers from the bar. It is *extremely* laid back and the endemic surfers have a reputation for being snotty and territorial. So!

Golfito

The Austrian-run **Esquinas Rain Forest Lodge**, a fine place that's popular with serious eco-adventurers, is near Golfito (see *Best Sleeps*). Unless you're going there, avoid this sleazy little town at all costs.

Zancudo

The name is local dialect for "mosquito," and these and surfers are about all you'll find here. Vultures lazily chew carcasses in the middle of the main street, a rutted dirt track. The only reason to come here is to stay at **Roy's Zancudo Lodge** (see *Best Sleeps*), an excellent and colorful fishing lodge.

11. BEST SLEEPS & EATS

HOTELS

Costa Rica has a full range of different types of lodgings. You can stay in a concrete-and-glass tower in a hermetically sealed big city hotel tower block, or in a jungle cabina with no solid walls - just a floor, roof, screens and you and the toucans. You can luxuriate at an all-inclusive beachfront resort with a championship golf course and an elaborate pool, or be an ecotourist at a remote tropical ecology research station where scientists show visitors how they study the mating habits of howler monkeys.

I have selected **the best hotels and lodges of several types,** modern to rustic, moderate to stratospherically expensive, and I describe them here for you to make your selection, according to the type of travel that interests you.

All of the hotels listed here are more or less up to North American standards, with a few notable exceptions. Some are luxurious by international standards, some are interesting for other reasons.

Expect some of the more remote lodges to lack air conditioning,

electricity or hot water. The only way to make a phone call may be via a super-expensive satellite link.

Insects are a part of everyday life in the tropics in even the most hygienic establishments. I'm never surprised to find a stray bug or two in even the snobbiest places in the country. Bugs happen.

Remember that you don't necessarily need to worry about how to get to your lodge. Some of the remote ones are very complicated to find on your own, but a piece of cake if you let them make travel arrangements for you. Most are happy to arrange transport from the airport to their door, as well as lining up guides for local tours and activities.

Prices shown are for two people in one room during high season, usually including tax. Rooms have private bath unless otherwise noted.

EATING OUT

Restaurants in Costa Rica vary from local **open-air eateries** roasting chickens over an open fire (delicious!) to attempts at **world-class fine dining** with linen napkins and sorbet between courses (delicious!) and of course, everything in between. As a tourist or a short-term visitor you are offered a small but interesting range of eateries somewhere between these two extremes. Be sure to break out of the tourist herd a couple of times for a local *casado* plate lunch, and stop in at one of the finest tables in the country for a night of fine dining.

Expect to pay about the same prices you would pay in the US for restaurant meals. Expect meat, fish, pasta and vegetable meals like those served in the US, but think fresh. They don't use a lot of frozen stuff in Costa Rica, yet. The wonderful fresh seafood and flavorful tropical fruits are enough by themselves to satisfy any foodie. The **delicious Costa Rican coffee** alone is worth a trip!

Be aware that good hotels often have good restaurants. In many areas of the country, hotels and lodges are where you will find the fancy eats. Most lodges, even remote jungle lodges, are interested in having you come for dinner even if you are not a guest. Call first.

Typical Costa Rican cuisine (known as *comida típica*) is easy to find at local restaurants throughout the country, especially at the small cafés called *sodas*. Such restaurants are usually reasonably cheap, and can be quite good. A typical plate is called a *casado* (literally, "married"), and consists of a big piece of meat or fish, one or more vegetables (often a fried plantain and/or a pile of chopped cabbage), and a large helping of rice and beans. Many travelers give *comida típica* a bad rap, because the beans and rice (*gallo pinto*), served at all meals, can get boring, and because cooks tend to go heavy on the lard and the salt.

Fresh fish and seafood are excellent, but sadly not as readily available as you might like. Although seafood is found aplenty in Costa Rican waters, it tends to be expensive locally, as most of what is caught is exported. By no means all the seafood served is fresh. You know you're getting really fresh fish at a fishing lodge, or at a funky local beach shack where you see the cook buying from a local fisherman. At that touristy restaurant in San José or Monteverde, however, you are likely to be presented with an unspectacular frozen fish or shrimp.

San José and, to a lesser extent, other cities, feature a range of restaurants including French, Italian, Chinese, Mexican and other worldwide favorites. Eateries in tourist areas serve American favorites such as burgers and pizza. The results can be very good, or they can be lame and overpriced.

In most of the country, your dining choices will be between hearty-but-monotonous *comida típica* and sometimes imperfectly executed international cuisine. In some of the finer resorts and wilderness lodges however, the style of cookery is so different from either of these options, and yet so uniquely Costa Rican, that I have elevated it to a separate category, which, for want of a better term, we shall call **resort cuisine** (or how about neo-Tico?).

Resort cuisine is based on fresh local ingredients, but influenced by the modern North American and European cooking tradition, with its emphasis on low-fat cooking and healthy ingredients, and by a cosmopolitan mix of the world's cuisines, particularly Eastern ones. This happy culinary marriage is the result of two trends. Many lodge operators are from Europe, where cooking is a fine art, and they are familiar with world cuisines including

Costa Rican Dishes *(comida típica)*

agua dulce - sweet, hot water consumed like coffee or tea

arreglados - greasy pastries with meat or cheese

arroz con leche - rice pudding

arroz con pollo - fried rice with chicken

batido - fruit smoothie made with either milk or water and ice

bocas - snacks, usually served in bars to accompany beer inducing patrons to buy even more beer to go with the *bocas*

casado – The archetypal Costa Rican dish is a plate lunch (or dinner) consisting of a choice of meat or fish with a large number of vegetable side items usually including plantains, rice, beans, cabbage, corn, and fruit. A *casado* is usually the best way to sample local food at reasonable prices.

casava - a large, potato-like root vegetable with a fairly plain flavor

ceviche - marinated seafood, "cooked" by lime juice, not by heat

chan - a strange slimy drink made from weird seeds

chorreados - corn pancakes usually with sour cream

chuleta - chop

chicharones - fried pork skins

coyol - palm wine, exceedingly dangerous

elote - corn on the cob

empanadas - turnovers with beans, cheese, meat, or potatoes

enchiladas - pastries with cheese and potatoes or meat

gallo pinto - "Spotted rooster" is usually served at breakfast and consists of last night's leftover rice and beans stir fried with garlic, onions and whatever is on hand. Delicious!

guaro - *very potent* local hooch made from sugar

hígado en salsa - liver in sauce

horchata - a cinnamon-flavored drink made with corn or rice

mondongo - soup made from beef stomach

olla de carne - beef stew

palmitos - heart of palm

patacones - fried plantains

pinolillo - a hot drink made from chocolate and corn

plantain - a large, fat, unsweet banana usually fried and served with meals.

queque - cake

resbaladera - a drink made from barley and rice

tres leches - a sweet cake drenched in sweet milk, delicious!

Chinese, Japanese, Thai and Indian. Most visitors are affluent Americans and Europeans who are accustomed to a light, health-conscious style of cooking, and who find typical Costa Rican fare, with its emphasis on meat and overcooked vegetables, to be unhealthful (many Costa Rican lodges cater specifically for health-conscious travelers).

In expert hands, the results can be delightful. The most memorable meals I've had in Costa Rica fall into this category. A hypothetical dinner, served buffet-style, might include things like: chicken marinated with fresh papayas and mangos and grilled; chicken or lean beef lightly stir-fried with ginger and sesame; a medley of fresh vegetables, lightly cooked and still crispy, with a hint of curry; salad with hearts of palm in a balsamic vinaigrette sauce; cilantro chutney; fresh local fish, grilled with fresh vegetables; another type of fish, prepared as a *ceviche*; mango pie and other fruit-based desserts. Some lodges that execute this culinary tradition well are **Silver King Lodge** in Barra del Colorado, and **Iguana Lodge** in the Peninsula de Osa.

No Costa Rican meal is complete without a dash of *Lizano* sauce. You'll find a bottle of this delicious tamarind-based condiment on the table at every restaurant. Vaguely similar to Worcestershire (but lighter) or to the Jamaican Pickapeppa, *salsa Lizano* makes the perfect companion to *gallo pinto*, but goes well with almost any savory dish. Ticos go through the stuff by the gallon, and the founder of the company that makes it is said to be one of Costa Rica's richest men.

Costa Rican **coffee** is excellent. I like a *café con leche*, which tends to be about half milk. If you want black coffee, ask for *café negro*. Beer is brewed in the German lager tradition. Local brands such as **Imperial** (*águila* in local slang) and the hearty **Bavaria** are very good. Wine is, of course, not produced in the tropics, so most Costa Ricans aren't big wine drinkers. Imported wine (often from Chile) is available in stores and at upscale restaurants, but it's expensive, and the selection is usually limited.

Rum, distilled from sugar, is the typical tropical liquor. There's a variety of brands available, ranging from basic mixing rum to fine, dark sipping rum. Rum and Coke (*Cuba Libre*) is Costa Rica's most popular mixed drink. Some of the locals drink *guaro*, a clear liquor distilled from sugarcane. Similar to moonshine or to Jamaican "overproof" rum, guaro is very cheap and very strong. You have been warned.

San José
Sleeps

Whatever you eat in Costa Rica, do not neglect to sample some of whatever fruits are in season. The mangos, pineapples, papayas, bananas, citrus and other tropical delights that grow down here are simply different fruits from the ones you buy at the supermarket back home: sweet, juicy and cheap. Fresh-squeezed juices from a rainbow of exotic fruits are available everywhere. Don't be afraid to experiment.

SAN JOSÉ & THE CENTRAL VALLEY

BEST SLEEPS IN SAN JOSÉ

Most people who come to enjoy the tropical delights of Costa Rica arrive at the Juan Santamaría International Airport just outside San José on afternoon flights, without enough time to catch a local flight to their ultimate jungle, beach or other destination. Most internal flights leave in the morning to avoid afternoon cloud cover. This usually means a night spent more or less near the airport.

Although San José does have its attractions, in general one shouldn't feel guilty about blowing it off for more interesting places. San José has lots of great hotels and restaurants but it tends to be noisy and exceedingly urban. There is not really much tropical charm.

Fortunately, the suburbs and the Central Valley around San José are much more laid-back and jungly, and are loaded with good places to stay and eat. Some of the best are conveniently near the airport for those who just need a place to stay overnight between planes. To enjoy the pleasures of the Central Valley, a lodge or hotel somewhat out of San José can be a good base for several days of exploration. If you find you must stay in downtown San José then here you are:

Hotel Grano De Oro $$$

The Grano de Oro is truly a beautiful, unique hotel with loads of charm, and is very professionally run. The location is central, but it's on a quiet side street, so you miss most of the city noise and traffic. This is my first choice for a place to stay in town. It is a member of the Small Distinctive Hotels of Costa Rica trade association.

The rooms and suites are especially private. There is a luxurious suite near the roof with a large Jacuzzi and **spectacular views of the city** and surrounding mountains. Rooms are all unique – this is not a chain – this is a charming, boutique hotel with lots of character built in and around an old coffee baron's home, a maze of atriums and greenhouses with thousands of potted tropical plants, and lots of wrought iron and damask. Costa Rican artists handcrafted the art and furnishings.

The restaurant is simply the **best restaurant in town**, tending towards French with tropical infusions, orchestrated by Chef Francis Canal. The desserts are famous. The giftshop, although not large, is one of the better ones in San José. *Info:* www.hotelgranodeoro.com. Tel. 255-3322. Calle 30, Avenidas 2/4.

Aurola Holiday Inn $$$

Right smack downtown, the Aurola is a modern glass tower, and bills itself as "your business center in Costa Rica." It's pretty much a regular **big city Holiday Inn** like what you would find in the US, with all the amenities expected by global business travelers. The hotel is currently undergoing extensive renovations in preparation for a rumored new franchisee.

The rooms come with everything you would expect to find in a modern city hotel anywhere: hair dryer, safe, iron, etc. (wireless internet is coming soon). The beds are great, with new mattresses and nice bedclothes. There is a small rooftop pool and exercise facility. Both are scheduled for major updates.

The rooms on the upper floors have tremendous views of San José and the surrounding volcanoes. The location is right downtown,

only a couple of blocks from Avenida and Calle Central. *Info:*
www.aurolahotels.com. Tel. 523-1000. 5th Avenue & 5th Street.

Hotel Del Rey $$$

The five-story Neoclassical Hotel del Rey is listed as a **National
Heritage Treasure**, but it's world famous for more than its
architecture. It is a clean, medium-quality hotel with elevator and
central air. The ground floor bustles with a 24-hour casino, a
crummy coffee shop/restaurant, and the more than lively bar.

The Del Rey is the San José stopover for guys on fishing junkets,
and is the most popular hotel for men looking to hire women for
an evening or longer. This is the best place in town to immerse
yourself in the **fleshy pleasures** (legal in Costa Rica) of San José.

At first glance, the **Blue Marlin Bar** beside the lobby is just a
pleasant, US-style sports bar with reasonably priced drinks. But
it won't take you long to notice the dozens (hundreds on the
weekends) of freelance ladies of the evening hanging about. You
have to see it to believe it, but leave the family in Carbondale. You
can check out the action live from home on their webcam
(www.hoteldelrey.com/webcam/index.html). The rooms are
okay too. *Info:* www.hoteldelrey.com. Tel. 257-7800, 800/971-
2451 US. Avenida 1, Calle 9.

Hotel Britannia $$

Conveniently located at the edge of downtown in pleasant Barrio
Amón, the Britannia is comfortable and moderately priced. It still
has much of the charm of the **old coffee baron's house** that forms
part of the complex of rooms.

Some of the rooms are a little on the small side, and the AC is
better in some than in others. The newer section actually has the
smaller rooms and the not-so-efficient air conditioning. All the
rooms have safes, phones and TV. The wireless internet access
works in the lobby and some of the rooms. The restaurant
downstairs is pleasant, with very carefully prepared food and a
pretty good wine list.

This is the best choice if you want to be really close to downtown but slightly out of the bustle. It's one of my favorites. *Info:* www.hotelbritanniacostarica.com. Tel. 223-6667. Calle 3, Avenida 11, Barrio Amón.

BEST SLEEPS NEAR SAN JOSÉ

Attractive alternatives to city hotels are found in the villages and valleys and on the mountains and volcanic slopes around San José. Although surrounded by fruit orchards, coffee plantations and rain forests, the inns and lodges of the Central Valley are only minutes from downtown San José, and many are just a short ride from the international airport.

Having just said that, I may as well warn you that traffic between the airports and San José can be incredibly slow. There's a back road from Heredia to the Airport that's much quicker (20 to 25 minutes with moderate traffic).

Casa Turire $$$$

A member of **Small Distinctive Hotels of Costa Rica**, this hotel is a great base for exploring Braulio Carillo National Park, as well as nearby volcanoes, horseback riding or whitewater rafting. With a long, palm-lined entry drive, this is one of the most elegant hotels in the country.

The 12 rooms and four suites feature graceful colonial-style décor, and luxury amenities such as hair dryers and private balconies. The restaurant serves Mediterranean cuisine with local organic ingredients and specialty items. It is heavy with white linen and glassware.

Casa Turire has extensive grounds, tennis courts, a lovely spring-fed pool, and even a heliport. It is reasonably close to Irazú volcano and the rather tame ruins at Guayabo National Monument. Located **right on the Reventazón River**, it would be a good luxury base for river rafting. *Info:* www.hotelcasaturire.com. Tel. 531-1111. Near Turialba.

Finca Rosa Blanca Country Inn $$$$

Gaudi and Timothy Leary must have inspired the architects for this unique, free-form white stucco property. "Elegant, yet whimsical," Finca Rosa Blanca is a very special luxury country inn in the coffee-covered hills not far outside San José. Sophisticated travelers will appreciate the attention to detail and over-the-top amenities.

If you don't mind spending for luxury and something different, you'll find Finca Rosa Blanca to be one of the nicest and most interesting places to stay in the Central Valley. There don't seem to be any square corners or regular windows. Every item has been created individually by hand — no two doors are alike. It's fun, elegant, and small enough to be intimate.

Dinners are prepared and served by advance request only, and are not to be missed. Finca Rosa Blanca is one of only two hotels that have earned the Costa Rican Tourist Board's highest rating for sustainable tourism, five green leaves. They grow their own organic coffee for the enjoyment of guests. *Info:* www.fincarblanca.co.cr. Tel. 269-9392. Santa Bárbara de Heredia.

Intercontinental Real Costa Rica $$$$
The Intercontinental is the nicest of the big-city, full-service hotels in Costa Rica. It is large, modern, luxurious, and has **every business convenience** expected.

The rooms are extremely comfortable and fully furnished without seeming plush - things are understated in a business-oriented way. Suites and special services floors offer world-class quality. There are several good restaurants with over-the-top buffets. The lobster buffet is legendary, with usually more than six styles of preparation including the usual grilled, steamed, thermidor, bisque, and on and on. The buffet with a glass of wine or two and coffee runs about $50 per person, but you do get to eat all of the lobster you can honk down.

The pool is huge and there is a fully equipped spa. Meeting rooms are set in the "forest" near the pool and have all the technical amenities needed for a major business conference. *Info:* www.interconti.com. Tel. 208-2100, 888/424-6835 US. Autopista Próspero Fernandez, San Antonio de Escazú.

Resort Martino $$$

This resort is located across the street from the delightful Zoo Ave just outside Alajuela, convenient to the airport. Operated by an Italian hotelier, it's a friendly, comfortable, well-run establishment. The large and beautifully landscaped grounds are a peaceful oasis.

The 34 modern, spacious rooms have every convenience, including phone, satellite TV, air conditioning and more. The buildings were constructed with imagination, and are filled with exotic woods crafted into unique interiors and furnishings.

There's an enormous **pool, gym, spa,** conference center and tennis courts. The spa is one of the largest and nicest in the country. The Italian-style restaurant has good food and a nice terrace view. *Info:* www.hotelmartino.com. Tel. 433-8382, 866/ 272-7477 US. La Garita de Alajuela.

Hotel Alta $$$

A Mediterranean **architectural masterpiece**, the Alta is a joy to visit. Stucco, arches and wrought iron compliment verdant tropical landscaping. The lobby and public areas are filled with exhibits of art from local artists. The views are great and it is in a quiet area. It's a bit on the wrong end of town for the international airport, but good for Escazú.

The 23 rooms have all the conveniences expected in a first-class hotel, including internet access, direct-dial phones, minibar, coffee maker, work desk and safe. Tile floors open onto nice balconies or patios, some with panoramic views of the mountains.

The restaurant is one of the most interesting in Costa Rica, specializing in Pacific Rim fusion with local fish and fruit. The wine list and selections at the bar are noble. *Info:* www.thealtahotel.com. Tel. 282-4160, 888/388-2582 US. West of Escazú on the old road to Santa Ana.

The White House $$$

With new owners and refurbishment, the White House is a classy and unique place to stay, full of character and style. Not too long ago the White House was known as Tara and filled an interesting slot in Costa Rica's social life as The Place for **society weddings**. It was famous for its US-style southern charm with a *Gone With the Wind* theme. It is still a great choice. The theme now is US Presidential. You are the Commander in Chief during your stay. Rooms are named after former US presidents.

The hotel is in a very large home built as a refuge for the Shah of Iran who never had the opportunity to stay there (visa problems). Each room is different, with antique furniture and period rugs. The views are out over the valley towards Escazú and feature three volcanoes. The immediate neighborhood is perhaps not as nice as the hotel itself, so you may wake up to the sounds of chickens cackling and dogs barking. The restaurant is based around truly lavish buffets. *Info:* www.whitehousecostarica.com. Tel. 228-6362, 954/272-8566 US. Escazú.

Hampton Inn $$$
This hotel is very close to the airport, and is the usual well-run Hampton Inn like the ones you may have stayed at in the US, with air-conditioning, cable TV, alarm clocks and a passable fruit and cereal breakfast buffet. It's not exactly luxury but it's **comfortable, modern and familiar** with all the expected in-room goodies.

If you are just changing planes and don't want to go into San José, this is a good spot to stay over. It's about a $12 taxi ride into downtown, and perhaps $2 to the airport. In fact, the airport is close enough that you could walk if you felt like it. *Info:* www.hamptonhotel.co.cr. Tel. 442-3320.

Debbie King's Country Inn $$
This colorful inn offers the best of both worlds, with tranquility and the sounds of nature just 10 minutes from town. The inn is perched on **three acres of fruit and coffee**, with incredible views of the volcano and city lights. It's 20 minutes from the airport and 10 minutes from Heredia.

Prices range from $60 for lovely upper inside double rooms with awesome views to $80 for private guesthouses (2 to 6 persons) with fully equipped kitchens and private baths (extra person

$20). Owner Debbie will assist you with all tour arrangements. This is a great place for home base because of its tranquility and close proximity to all attractions. It's **my favorite place to stay in the Central Valley**.

Debbie's is not only economical but probably one of the friendliest places you will ever stay besides grandma's house. British expat Debbie King keeps things just so, in a very English way. Her parlor feels like **a little bit of England** right here in Costa Rica. Rooms, some with kitchens, come with everything you need to make tea, including a typical electric kettle.

Besides all this, Debbie is a blast and keeps keyboards and guitar on hand and in tune, in case any guests feel like a jam session. Debbie is an actress and used to have a celebrity-frequented restaurant (DK's) in Hollywood. From time to time some of her famous buddies come and stay. I could tell some stories about playing guitar, singing, and enjoying relaxing beverages until late at night on Debbie's porch with an international rock group on vacation, but I have been sworn to secrecy. *Info:* www.freewebs.com/debbieking. Tel. 268-3084, 380-8492. Just outside Heredia.

Pura Vida Hotel $$
Comfortable, homey, yet private, the Hotel Pura Vida is **very convenient to the airport** and a good place to stop and explore the Central Valley. Poás and the coffee tours are just around the corner. The hotel has several *casitas*, or small houses, with **kitchens**, good reading lights and all the comforts of home. You can brew up a cup of wonderful coffee as soon as you get to your room. Friendly dogs will help you get settled in, if you like. The gardens are filled with an astonishing variety of flowering things. There is a small orchid garden.

You can rely on owners Berni and Nhi to help with your touring plans. Because of their location near the airport, they often get visitors stopping in for a night before heading off to other parts of the country and then stopping by again at the end of their trips for a night before flying out. Over the years they have become good at helping people plan and arrange their time in the country to best advantage. They are friendly people and can be quite

Vacation Lodgings

If you plan to stay in one place for a week or more, **renting a guest house** may be an economical and comfortable alternative to staying at a hotel. Local real estate agencies have lots of vacation rentals available, from moderately-priced apartments to luxurious seaside villas. Use one of the Costa Rica-based search engines to find a local agent in the region you're interested in (see Websites, near the end of the *Practical Matters* chapter).

One caveat about renting a place: what you see on a web site and what you find when you arrive may be two different things (alas, the same applies to hotels, although not, of course, to the ones listed in this book). Be sure to ask plenty of questions, and search online to see if there are any comments from other travelers who've rented through a particular real estate agent in the past.

These sites have links to available rentals in all price ranges, throughout the country:
- www.viviun.com/Rentals/Costa_Rica
- www.goin2travel.com/costa-rica-vacation-rentals.htm
- www.cyberrentals.com/Costa-Rica/r1021.htm
- www.costaricaweeklyvacationrentals.com
- If price is no object, check out some of the beautiful properties at: www.unusualvillarentals.com/costa-rica.

helpful. They have a good driver and van service available if you need transport into San José or to almost anywhere in the country.

This is **one of my favorites**. Be sure to get in on one of their fabulous dinners. They don't cook every night, only on special request, so be sure to sort out a meal before you arrive. There is also a wonderful local seafood joint a short taxi ride away. *Info:* www.puravidahotel.com. Tel. 430-2630, 383-2597. Alajuela (2 miles from the international airport).

BEST SLEEPS NORTH OF SAN JOSÉ
Selva Verde Lodge $$
This **ecotourism center** right on the Sarapiquí River features a small botanical garden and a number of marked trails on the property. Just across the river is primary rain forest. It is waaay out in the jungle.

The River Lodge has open rooms on elevated platforms, with nice open wooden verandahs. The newer Bungalow rooms have AC and screened-in balconies.

Iguanas hang out by the pool, and you might just see a new bird from the bar or the beautiful porch overlooking the stream. Their nighttime jungle walk might require a couple of cups of coffee first, but is well worth the effort. Hiking, whitewater rafting and serious birding are high on the menu of activities. A complimentary bird watching walk is offered twice a day. *Info:* www.holbrooktravel.com/selvaverdelodge. Tel. 766-6800, 800/451-7111 US. Chilamate, Sarapiquí (about two hours north of San José).

BEST EATS - SAN JOSÉ & THE CENTRAL VALLEY
Here you'll find the country's most cosmopolitan selection of restaurants, from various international cuisines to local specialties, and delightful fusions of the two.

La Luz $$$$
La Luz is an upscale restaurant in the Hotel Alta in Escazú, with an excellent wine list and an imaginative menu. Seafood, steaks and chicken cooked with **Mediterranean and Asian influences** lead to some interesting combinations likely to upset traditionalists but please the palate. The wine list and bar selection are outstanding. *Info:* Tel. 282-4160. In the Hotel Alta, west of Escazú on the old road to Santa Ana.

Restaurante Grano de Oro $$$
This hotel restaurant has **the best table in San José**. Continental tradition mixed with Costa Rican seafood and produce ensure wonderful tasting, creative dishes. Desserts are singular. The setting is romantic, with potted tropical plants. *Info:* 255-3322. Calle 30, Avenidas 2/4. In the Hotel Grano de Oro.

Île de France $$$

Located in L'Hôtel de Bergerac, you should expect *entrecote*, *vichysoisse* and other French-influenced items. *Info:* Tel. 283-5812.

Restaurant Le Gourmet $$$

Located in the Hotel Martino just outside Alajuela, Le Gourmet features **traditional Italian cuisine** utilizing local produce, seafood and steaks and overlooks the classical pool and gardens. If you hanker for **gnocchi, veal or scampi**, this is one of the best in the country. It's a little formal but not at all uncomfortable. **This is a favorite**. *Info:* Tel. 433-8382. La Garita de Alajuela.

Vishnu $$

Convenient to downtown, Vishnu is a good spot for a **vegetarian** health-food meal at almost any time of day. It is a popular place with locals, and you'll see plenty of middle-class, **healthy young Ticas** scarfing up vegetarian chow. The smoothies are intense. *Info:* Tel. 222-2549. San José, Avenida 1, near Calle 3.

Marisquería Princesa Marina $$

The Princesa has several locations around San José, including one in Alajuela and one in Escazú. It is a good place to **honk down a big pile of shrimp** or **inexpensive lobster**. For under $10 you can gorge on them along with all the usual seafood items. Wine and beer are basic and good. This is one of my favorite places to eat. *Info:* Tel. 232-0481.

La Casona de Cerdo BBQ & Chicharronera $$

If you turn on the road that goes off in front of the Hampton Inn near the airport towards San José, after about two miles you'll come to a **top-quality BBQ emporium** complete with a huge stuffed pig in the entry. This is serious pork country, and a popular place with locals. It looks really busy when you drive up but the parking attendants will help you get in and out with little fuss. It's a big place and there is seldom much of a line. *Info:* Near Heredia on Rió Segundo Road.

NORTH CARIBBEAN COAST

BEST SLEEPS IN PARISMINA

There is not much reason to come to Parismina except for fishing, but that's more than enough to draw thousands of visitors each year from all over the world to this remote, nothing little village. The tarpon and snook fishing are world-class, and **Tortuguero National Park** begins just north of the inlet. The Tortuguero Canal, the main means of travel in the north Caribbean, runs right through "town." There are two excellent fishing lodges. Guides are available for organized turtle worship on the beaches at night when they come ashore to lay eggs.

Río Parismina Lodge $$$

Judy Heidt has been running what is arguably the **most famous fishing lodge** in Costa Rica for more than 20 years. The rooms are comfortable (**free laundry service**), the food outstanding and the fishing fleet one of the best on the coast. Most of her guides have been with her for at least a decade. You can get to the lodge from San José by bus and boat, if flying to isolated runways in small planes isn't your thing.

This is a serious fishing lodge, but there is still plenty to do for non-fishing guests. All the usual tours are available, with turtle worship at the nearby **Tortuguero National Park** a specialty. Few people come to this end of the park to visit, so you avoid the crowds. There is a nice pool and Jacuzzi.

Coffee is brought right to your door every morning at 5:00 and a lavish breakfast buffet with freshly baked pastries and piles of tropical fruits is presented. If you move quickly, you can be fighting a tarpon by 6 am. After fishing, the booze flows as freely as you like, accompanied by delicious *bocas* and the usual fishy conversation. Judy is a superb hostess and holds several world records herself.

Expect to fish more with live bait and circle hooks than with lures. **Snook fishing** at the mouth of the inlet is done both by slow trolling and casting from the shore. I admit I've never personally caught anything surf fishing but enthusiasts swear the biggest snook are caught this way. *Info:* www.riop.com. Tel. 800/338-5688 US.

Jungle Tarpon Lodge $$
Smaller than the other lodges, but with air-conditioning and all the other mod cons, Jungle Tarpon Lodge is quiet, comfortable and efficient. There are four large guest rooms and a screened-in lounge/dining area. There is a small but well-equipped bar with drinks included in most packages. Expect personal service and great Costa Rican food.

The lodge makes a real effort to entertain non-fishing guests, with the usual eco-tours into the forest by small boat and on foot. Walks on the beach at night to observe turtles laying eggs in season can be arranged through the nearby **Tortuguero National Park.**

Circle hooks and **live bait** are the norm here, ensuring more **tarpon** actually getting to the boat for release. When not using live bait, tarpon are caught trolling plugs or casting seahawks in the lagoon. When the river mouth is passable, live bait or bottom-bumping seahawks are cast into schools of tarpon that at times cover several acres. There are thousands and thousands of tarpon out there. The lodge is quite close to the main fishing areas. Boats and tackle are newish and well maintained. There is some fly fishing equipment on hand but hard-core fly anglers should bring their own goodies. *Info:* www.jungletarpon.com. Tel. 800/544-2261 US.

BEST SLEEPS IN TORTUGUERO
Tortuguero is all about turtles, jungle cruises and hikes through **Tortuguero National Park.** Lodges line the canal near the airport and the charmingly tiny and not-quite-grubby village. **Tortuga Lodge** is the best. **Laguna** and **Mawamba** are also very nice.

The village itself has a couple of small backpacker lodgings and a couple of *sodas* where you can arrange for seafood dinners at reasonable prices. Some small tour operators have offices in the village. There is quite a nice gift shop by the main dock. You can see the gigantic plastic toucan in front from far away announcing the type of things on offer inside.

Tortuga Lodge $$
This is the nicest lodge in the area. The comfortable and clean rooms are in a two-story motel-style building, and have all the modern conveniences (no TVs or phones, though). The food leans toward **local seafood** and is served communally on long tables in a screened-in room overlooking the river, a peaceful place to compare notes with other travelers. The pool is small but refreshing after a long day visiting the nearby park or fishing.

Tortuga lodge is one of the ones operated by **Costa Rica Expeditions**, and they run a tight, well-managed ship. Guides and tours can be arranged through the lodge, and utilize the lodge's own dedicated guides, who are trained and certified by Costa Rica Expeditions.

Although not primarily a fishing destination, Tortuguero has tarpon and snook fishing just about as good as you can find anywhere. Guides such as world-famous **Captain Eddie Brown** (Tel. 383-6097, 382-3350) operate from the lodge and can take you for an unforgettable angling experience. *Info:* www.tortugalodge.com. Tel. 257-0766, 222-0333, 800/948-3770 US.

Laguna Lodge $$
On the beach side of the canal, Laguna is aimed mostly at large groups of **package tourists** being herded from San José or from cruise ships docking in nearby Limón. The flower-filled grounds and pool are beautiful, and they have well-organized tours of all types. The rooms are air-conditioned, with safes and the usual amenities. There are no TVs in the rooms. No problem. The beach is wild, sandy with lots of driftwood and not suitable for swimming but **great for walks**.

The buffets are good, with steak, chicken, fish, a few local specialties and all the usual tourist vegetables and fruit. The big breakfast buffet includes pancake and omelet stations. The bartenders are cheerful and pour liberally, and you can sit right at the edge of the river and sip your umbrella drink watching the birds and crocs go by.

The lodge is well managed and comfortable. The main buildings, restaurant and bar are built in a wild, Gaudiesque style with free-form railings and soaring rooflines. Live entertainment in the bar before dinner is quite touristy, often resulting in spontaneous conga lines sashaying into the buffet. Guests are divided up into groups of 10 or so and encouraged to eat together, and are assigned to the same guides for the duration of their stay. This way you get to make friends and get to know the guides a bit. Call for specials. *Info:* www.lagunatortuguero.com. Tel. 272-4943, 709-8082.

Mawamba Lodge $$
Also on the beach side, Mawamba exudes **tropical ambiance**. The large and extravagant pool ensures kids will have plenty to do. This is a good base for exploring the nearby park in small boats and turtle worship on the beach. Like the Laguna Lodge, it is right on both the river and the dramatic beach. Walks on the beach are spectacular, but it's way too rough for safe swimming. Most guests are on package deals that include tours and meals.

The jungle cruises are famous up and down the river. Buffets are the usual tourist fare with tropical fruits and local specialties. The same company operates the wonderful **Trogon Lodge** near Cerro de La Muerte. *Info:* www.grupomawamba.com. Tel. 293-8181, 223-2421.

BEST SLEEPS IN BARRA DEL COLORADO
Barra del Colorado consists of two shabby villages on either side of the river near the inlet and three wonderful fishing lodges. There is no action here whatsoever except for fishing and exploring the nearby park. The beaches are wild and rough. The inlet is well known for being home to bull sharks and crocodiles as well as huge tarpon and snook.

The three lodges below differ slightly in their prices and services—but not much. All are **wonderful places to stay**, and you are just about as likely to catch loads of fish at one as at the others.

North
Caribbean
Sleeps

All three are dripping with tropical fishing lodge charm. All three are quite comfortable.

The **food at these lodges is legendary**. These are three of the best places to eat in the entire country. The anglers who come from all over the world for the unique fishing are paying huge amounts of money for the privilege and tend to be high-earning executives, trust fund babies and wealthy entertainers accustomed to wining and dining in the finest restaurants of the world. They expect similar cuisine when they fish. These lodges supply both the world-class cuisine and the world-class tarpon and snook fishing required.

Any of the lodges in the area will arrange your entire trip from the time you leave home until you arrive, ready to fish. This is a good option, as the only way to get here is by small plane and boat.

Skip Samay!

The former **Samay Lagoon Lodge**, located outside Barra del Colorado, is closed and has fallen into disrepair. There are reports of rip-off attempts operating out of the old rotting shell under the names Samal Lodge and Kahlua Lodge. A few unfortunate anglers have fallen for the pitch and had to abort their holidays due to the inability of what is left of the lodge to deliver the goods.

Silver King Lodge $$$
Silver King has not only the best boats and guides but also the nicest rooms and pool in the area. Their food is some of the best I've eaten anywhere in Costa Rica. The groaning morning, noon and evening buffets are filled with dozens of meats, fish and **gourmet specialties** better than a dozen grandmas or French chefs could make.

The service is really special. As you step off your boat every evening you are handed an amazing frozen tropical cocktail and directed to the pool and **Jacuzzi**, where snacks and more drinks await. Any clothes you drop on the floor are washed and placed back in your room daily. Every night before bedtime, there is a tap at the door and you are presented with an insulated pitcher of ice water.

The lodge makes its own boats and uses top-quality gear. The boats are well outfitted with all the modern fishing electronics as seen on TV. Even more important, the local guides know how to put you onto the fish.

Fanatical anglers who buy fishing magazines and watch the fishing shows on Saturday morning TV know that the Caribbean side of Costa Rica offers the world's top tarpon and snook fishing. **Tarpon over 100 pounds** school up in their thousands off the river mouths and over sandy bottoms offshore. **Snook over 20 pounds** are caught surf fishing near the river mouths or by trolling and casting in lagoons. The Silver King Lodge is where those fishing fanatics would like to be right now. *Info:* www.silverkinglodge.com. Tel. 381-1403, 381-0849, 800/847-3474 US.

Río Colorado Lodge $$$

An old Mississippi charmer, Dan Wise is a **genial host,** and tells some of the most preposterous, but perhaps true, fishing stories you'll hear anywhere. The lodge is old and funky but comfortable and **full of character.** The rooms are well appointed, with individual air-conditioning, good reading lights and hot water. The food tends toward down-home Southern specialties with plenty of seafood and Dan's grandmother's **fried chicken** recipe.

Equipment is top-notch and the guides very experienced. This lodge is the closest one to the action. Many record-breaking fish have been caught here, including a world-record **machaca,** landed from their dock using a banana for bait.

Hanging around the dock and bar at Río Colorado for conversation and lies after fishing all day is one of life's great pleasures. This is **one of my favorite places to stay in the world.** Río Colorado's package deals are hard to beat. *Info:* www.riocoloradolodge.com. Tel. 232-4063, 232-8610, 800/243-9777 US.

Casa Mar Fishing Lodge $$$

This is the **oldest fishing lodge in the area,** dripping with atmosphere and charm, and the walls are covered with photographs of famous people next to gigantic fish. If you read the fishing magazines, you already know that this is the granddaddy of tarpon lodges. **Lefty Kreh, Hank Williams Jr.** and other celebrities are aficionados.

It is a bit far from the other lodges, but has an old-time charm all its own. Elvis, a black and tan **coonhound**, greets guests at the dock. Rooms are air-conditioned, and the manager, Lefty, does a good job making sure guests have everything they need.

Food is served in the main lodge and tends toward local fish and meat with piles of vegetables and fruit. Desserts are made fresh each day, and there is a large ice cream locker in the dining room. Guests are encouraged to dip in for a bowl or two of ice cream whenever the urge strikes.

The bar is excellent, and most of the packages include unlimited access to its charms. The last time I was there, there wasn't actually any bartender — guests just walked behind the bar and did their own thing. One guest who made wonderful margaritas found himself behind the bar performing his act every night. Boats and other fishing equipment are top-notch, and so are the local guides. **Fly fishermen** are catered to more here than at the other lodges. *Info:* www.casamarlodge.com. Tel. 433-9287, 433-8834, 800/543-0282 US.

BEST EATS ON THE NORTH CARIBBEAN COAST

The two regions of the Caribbean coast (north or south of Limón) are quite different, primarily because there are roads in the south and the only travel in the north is by boat or small plane. Consequently, almost all of the tourist facilities in the north are planned around all-inclusive resorts with little of interest going on in the small villages. **Dining in at your all-inclusive lodge is really the only option**. Most serve huge buffets with excellent resort cuisine and plenty to drink.

Bountiful Buffets

The **all-inclusive fishing lodges** in the north, such as Rió Parismina Lodge and Rió Colorado, offer **groaning buffets** of down-home and tropical cooking ten grandmas couldn't duplicate. The fresh fish, snook and snapper, will always be a star on those tables. The **dessert buffets** are dangerous.

SOUTH CARIBBEAN COAST

BEST SLEEPS IN CAHUITA
Selva Bananito Lodge $$
Located adjacent to **Parque International La Amistad** biosphere, Selva Bananito is one of the best places to learn about **tropical ecology**. This remote lodge was established at the edge of a cattle ranch run on low-impact principles, with over **2,000 acres left undisturbed**. Primary rain forest is one of the main draws for scientists and serious birders.

The accommodations are basic, but no one comes here for luxury. The proximity to unspoiled forest draws guests looking for outdoor activities and the opportunity to see an outstanding variety of wildlife, including over 300 species of birds. Ornithologists are on staff for consultation. The $220 rate includes all meals, taxes, transportation from Bananito, and some activities for two. *Info:* www.selvabananito.com. Tel. 253-8118.

No Nuts, Please

The glossy brochures and website make **Almonds and Corals** in the Gandoca Manzanillo Wildlife Refuge look like a tropical honeymoon paradise, but the reality is anything but. The tents are on platforms over a swamp, with little privacy and lots of mosquitoes. The restaurant is nothing special. There are no safes in the rooms, and the safe at the front desk is left open all day (and perhaps all night) as dozens of employees and others bustle around. Stinkpots emitting black smoke line the walkways at night to keep mosquitoes more or less at bay. There is a tacky and simple zip line on the grounds. There are many nicer places to stay nearby.

BEST SLEEPS IN PUERTO VIEJO
Funky, rustic and laid-back are some of the (kinder) adjectives applied to this little oceanfront village down near the Panamanian border. It features beautiful beaches, a bit of coral reef for snorkeling, and a colorful party scene. This area tends to attract surfers, backpackers and the granola set, rather than luxury travelers.

Cariblue Bungalow Hotel $$

This European-managed hotel is one of the nicest ones in the south. It's right across the street from **Playa Cocles**, a beautiful expanse of white sand and shady palm trees. It's an excellent surfing beach (the local nickname is "beach break"), but it also has calm areas that are good for swimming (and—a rarity— occasionally a lifeguard on duty).

The rooms are in typically tropical bungalows with thatched roofs. They have private bathrooms, ceiling fans and mosquito nets, but no AC. Hammocks tempt you to take an afternoon nap. There's also a house with a kitchen available for larger groups. The new pool nestles among lush vegetation, and features a swim-up bar. The restaurant is great, if a little expensive, with **huge seafood feasts**. *Info:* www.cariblue.com. Tel. 750-0035, 750-0518.

Villas del Caribe $$

For the price, this is one of the best bargains in the area. All the rooms have balconies and ceiling fans, and some have AC. There are also some two-level villas with all the goodies, including **kitchens**. They front right on the beach and some sleep up to eight people. There are dozens of palm trees dotted about and the beach is only a few feet away from the rooms. Puerto Viejo is a short bike ride away and there are a couple of small bars and such reasonably close by. The place is a little older and run-down but it still has charm. Avoid the restaurant if possible. *Info:* www.villasdelcaribe.com. Tel. 750-0202, 233-2200.

Turtles, Not Luxury

Don't expect luxury but do expect comfortable lodging convenient to beaches and outdoor attractions. Turtles and monkeys are the draw in the north, rather than discos and drinking. The south has more variety, and some people come specifically to enjoy the social aspects of the youth culture of surfing and fun that thrives in the area.

Cashew Hill Jungle Lodge $

This laid-back little lodge is up on a hill above Puerto Viejo, with a splendid view of Salsa Brava and Cahuita Bay. Friendly owners Erich

& Wendy Strebe bought the place in 2003 and have made several improvements. Cabinas with private baths and kitchen facilities go for $35-60 double. Groups of up to 18 people can rent the entire lodge. *Info:* www.cashewhilllodge.co.cr. Tel. 750-0256.

BEST EATS ON THE SOUTH CARIBBEAN COAST

South of Limón you can find funky local eateries with spicy, Caribbean-influenced food, as well as innovative tourist-oriented places with wonderful fresh seafood. It's a little hard to find really cheap eats. The tourist places are usually quite good but the prices may seem a little over the top. Cahuita and Puerto Viejo both have a couple of happening hot spots for spicy local specialties.

A growing tourist trade has spawned a crop of trendy places to try out interesting tropical/new-world fusions and a few especially interesting local joints remain and even improve. Fine dining has found its way to the south Caribbean coast of Costa Rica, to star alongside the Tico and Jamaican flavors already there. Seafood is almost always going to be a good thing to order.

Amimodo $$$
The Italian atmosphere just cannot be smothered by the tropical ambiance. Mama and Papa fuss over the place, shouting in Italian to the cook in the back. Local seafood and produce prepared with **Italian** style make for some interesting meals. The food is good but keep your eye on the bartender. *Info:* Tel. 750-0257. Just south of Puerto Viejo.

Cariblue $$$
It's a little expensive, but the seafood is great and the wine is Italian and not bad at all. The salads can be 6 inches high with all sorts of **seafood gems lurking within**. Scampi is a similar show.

Fish & Seafood Terms

To help you order your *pescado y mariscos:*
atún - **tuna, usually caught locally, don't miss it**
calmar - squid
camarón - shrimp
dorado - the fish also known as mahi-mahi or dolphin
langosta - lobster
pargo - snapper
pargo entero - whole snapper with head, eyes, bones, and all
robalo - snook

Wine comes in a large glass. No matter how hard I try to get a small meal here, I always end up with waaay more than I can eat and have to decide whether to leave some shrimp on my plate or skip dessert. Don't skip dessert. *Info:* Tel. 750-0035. South of Puerto Viejo in the Hotel Cariblue.

La Pecora Nera $$$

Yet another Italian restaurant serving up wonderful seafood, but this happens to be the **best restaurant on the whole Caribbean** south coast. Don't miss a meal here. Be sure to ask for specials. Lunch is always an option if things are crowded in the evening. Reservations are essential. When I stopped in for lunch one time, a local fisherman came into the restaurant with several **huge snapper** for sale. He left with a grin and a wad of banknotes in his pocket as the cook carried the fish into the back. The daily special suddenly became snapper. Delicious. *Info:* Tel. 750-0490. South of Puerto Viejo.

Don't Tell Anybody...

... but the really hip scene has moved down the road to **Puerto Viejo**. By the time you visit, **Manzanillo**, even further south, along towards Panama, will be the happening place. It's already great. But don't tell anybody.

Maxí's $$

Almost at the end of the road, in Manzanillo, a fishing village of just a few small houses, is Maxi's, a soulful restaurant that serves fresh fish, shrimp and **lobster**. This is the center of the (small) local scene. I like to grab a seat that overlooks the beach to sip beer, enjoy some people watching and eat a *pargo entero* (whole red snapper). This would be a good place to go to seed. *Info:* You can't miss it.

Edith's $$

All **vegetarian** and all authentic Caribbean, this is the best place in town for a combination of good, inexpensive and interesting. Your stomach needs to be up to the strong Caribbean flavors, though. Be prepared for **spicy food**. If you order fish you might get just that, with head, bones, and all.

Edith's is the most interesting place to eat on the south coast, and the namesake cook, who declares that "love is the most important ingredient," one of the most interesting people to meet. You have to stop here at least once. Typical of Jamaican restaurants, the service is excruciatingly slow. *Soon come. Info:* Tel. 755-0248. Cahuita.

NORTH-CENTRAL COSTA RICA

BEST SLEEPS IN FORTUNA/ARENAL
Tabacón Lodge $$$
This lodge is conveniently just up the street from the famous hot springs, but is said to be directly in the path of any serious Arenal eruption. The lodge is built on top of the lava flow from the last big one. **Pyroclastic flows** from new eruptions are scheduled to blast right through the valley, incinerating everything. Baked tourists, anyone?

The rooms are comfortable, but the restaurant has been getting poor reviews lately. The associated hot springs across the street are expensive, but room prices sometimes include access to the springs. *Info:* www.tabacon.com. Tel. 256-1500, 877/277-8291 US.

Arenal Observatory Lodge $$
Originally built as a research station for volcanologists, Arenal Observatory Lodge is the nicest place to stay in the area. Rooms are comfortable but basic, and some have **spectacular views** of the cone. They have a great pool and handicapped-accessible jungle trails. The

Boring Fortuna

Fortuna is an **uninteresting** tourism-support town, which is useful for booking tours if you don't have everything arranged before you get to the area. It's a little far from the volcano, and has no particular charms of its own. Most people prefer to stay somewhere closer to the volcano, where they might see some action if the clouds ever clear up. The interesting places to stay are on the way to the lake, towards the town of Nuevo Arenal and beyond. Most lodges can help you arrange any of the local tours and activities. Without a car, transportation can be a bit of a problem.

restaurant and bar are good, with a nice view, but are not really very exciting for the price.

The lodge is set in a heavily forested area with lots of **howler monkeys**. A very good **guided jungle walk** near the cone is included in the price. The howler monkeys wake you up in the morning if the volcano doesn't. This is a good base for exploring around the volcano, and is the closest hotel to the cone. The site is across a small valley from the main flow of lava and is therefore considered to be out of harm's way in the event of a major eruption. You're close to the action but presumably safe from random pyroclastic flows.

This lodge is **my favorite place to stay in the area**. I have heard reports lately that the direction of lava flow from the cone has changed, and that the nightly light shows put on by the volcano have shifted to the other side of the cone. You should check with the hotel before booking, or you may miss the performance. *Info:* www.arenal-observatory.co.cr. Tel. 290-7011, 692-2070.

BEST SLEEPS IN MONTEVERDE/SANTA ELENA
Monteverde Lodge $$$
Thousands of **bromeliads** infest the delightfully landscaped grounds around the most comfortable place to stay in Monteverde. With all the mod cons including AC, TV and phones, the rooms are contemporary and well maintained. This lodge is a little away from the dusty strip, and is quiet, with a wonderful view all the way down over the cloud forest slopes to the Pacific and Nicoya Peninsula.

This is one of several lodges run by **Costa Rica Expeditions**, which does a first-class job of arranging for **certified guides** to all the local places of interest. When I stay here, I simply put myself in their hands and let them make all my tour arrangements.

I found the tour prices to be the same as I would be likely to pay when not going through the lodge. I recently booked a tour through the lodge to Santa Elena at the price of $15 per person. In the morning when I met the guide I found that I was the only person going. When the wonderful tour was over the guide informed me that the price was $15. I know this is the going rate, but I doubled it since it lasted three hours and a little. I had assumed I would be paying for a personal guide if I were the only participant. The guide did a wonderful job helping me to see quetzals and three-wattled bellbirds.

The restaurant is expensive but very good. Seafood, steaks and chicken are creatively prepared. Be sure to try their *ceviche*. There is a good selection of Chilean and Spanish wines, with all price categories covered well. *Info:* www.costaricaexpeditions.com. Tel. 645-5126, 645-5057, 257-0766, 800/886-2609 US.

**Ecolodge San Luis
and Research Station $$**
If you are interested in **tropical ecology** and would like to rub shoulders with researchers and students, Ecolodge San Luis is the most interesting place to stay and explore the surrounding forest as well as the parks and sights around Monteverde. Twitchers and power birders love it, adding significantly to their life lists. Tourists with $700 titanium walking sticks and space-age water bottles rub shoulders with college professors and backpackers.

No Five Stars

The variety of lodging in the Monteverde/Santa Elena area is huge, and the comfort level runs from bunkhouses to quite comfortable. The quality level ends just before modest luxury. There are **no luxury lodges** or multi-star hotels.

The lodge is a little off the beaten path, but still very close to the park. In fact, it is a full-time **tropical biology research station**, operated by the University of Georgia, and almost always has students and instructors on site involved in various university-level tropical biology research projects. Guests are encouraged to participate. The atmosphere provided by having the students there, with classes and projects going on, makes for a refreshing break from the nearby tourist mania in Monteverde. The guides are usually students who take visitors to see their projects, on horseback rides, and on hikes through the cloud forest.

The food is great, but the rooms are Spartan. There is a choice between dormitory bunks, small cabins or individual rooms.

Prices vary, of course. The higher-priced rooms are comfortable if plain. There is hot water. If you are interested in serious ecological studies or just want to get the real low down on the area, this is the only place to stay. I like to stay outside Monteverde in the **Ecolodge San Luis** and drive in to town only when I have to. Prices include all meals and most activities. *Info:* www.ecolodgesanluis.com. Tel. 645-8049, 645-8051.

BEST SLEEPS IN RINCÓN

The Rincón area would be a good destination if you want to escape the tourist hordes of Monteverde/Arenal and enjoy rain forests and volcanoes without a crowd of other hikers on your heels. It's quite close to the international airport at Liberia, which might make a good alternative to flying into San José.

Hacienda-Lodge Guachipelín $$

Down-to-earth yet comfortable, this 50-room hotel is well situated to enjoy the attractions of the nearby park and the northern Guanacaste region of Costa Rica. It is located at the foot of Rincón de la Vieja volcano adjacent to the national park. Natural hot springs, rain forests, jungle waterfalls and volcanic mud pots are all close by. You can also enjoy the steam vents with their "unmistakable smell." A **four-hour hike to the crater** is offered every day.

The lodge is within a **working cattle ranch**, with large areas set aside for protection. This is a good place to stay if you are interested in **horseback** activities. They offer multi-day rides in the area around the park. There is a pool with natural spring water. Rooms with all meals and natural drinks run $130 for two. Not a bad deal. *Info:* www.guachipelin.com. Tel. 666-8075, 442-2818.

Nice Places, Some Bugs

Most visitors to the Arenal and Monteverde area don't come for luxury. They come to explore and learn about the rain and cloud forests and to see volcanoes, preferably erupting fairly vigorously. Expect musty jungle smells and bugs in what are otherwise nice places. In the jungle, the bugs have been winning the war since dinosaur days. Don't be surprised to find ants in even the cleanest and most well-run upscale lodgings.

Away From the Crowds

Rincón de la Vieja is a huge, semi-active volcanic mountain with at least nine bubbling craters. The national park of the same name is **little visited**, perhaps due to its isolation in the far north of the country, but is well worth a visit. If your interest is in seeing relatively unspoiled tropical rain and cloud forests, I suggest avoiding Monteverde and visiting Rincón instead. There are a few modestly comfortable places to stay. Over 350 bird species have been identified, including the three-wattled bellbird, great curassow, emerald toucanet, elegant trogon, blue-throated goldentail, spectacled owl, white-fronted amazon and guaco.

Rincón de la Vieja Mountain Lodge $$

This lodge is the closest one to the park, and one of the nicest places to stay in the area. The rustic wooden buildings are surrounded by lush rain forest. The lodge is run on ecologically friendly principles, with a small hydroelectric generator providing electricity 24 hours per day.

The 49 rooms are basic but comfortable, all with private bath, and some with bunk beds for families. Meals are served family-style in the restaurant. There's a small pool, a bar, a **zip line** on site and, surprise, dairy cows you can hang out with. Naturally, a huge variety of tours and activities in the region are on offer. *Info:* www.rincondelaviejalodge.net. Tel. 200-0238.

Rinconcito Lodge $

Located close to Rincón de la Vieja as well as Miravalles Volcano, Rinconcito ("little corner") is a small lodge specializing in organizing activities for guests including horseback riding, trips to **bubbling springs,** mud baths, boiling mud pots, hot springs, **waterfalls,** canopy tours, bird watching and other usual rain forest pursuits. Don't expect luxury at $30 per night for a double, but do expect comfort and adventure. The lodge offers transport to and from Liberia airport. *Info:* www.rinconcitolodge.com. Tel. 200-0074, 666-2764.

BEST EATS IN FORTUNA/ARENAL

This area is much more about nature and the cone than fine dining, so leave your gourmet at home and eat in your lodge, or try one of the great Tico *sodas* for a *casado*.

Rancho Paraíso Steak House $$

This is a proper steak house, nothing fancy but a really great selection of steaks including some from **Argentina**. Most of the steaks are a little tougher than what you would expect back home since most of the local beef is grass raised. The fancy stuff is exported, but the Rancho Paraíso has some good ones. Skip the house red. *Info:* Tel. 460-5333. On the way out of town towards the cone.

La Vaca Muca $

For a solid Costa Rican **casado**, or plate lunch/dinner, this is a winner. Your choice of beef, chicken, fish or other local specialty comes with countless vegetable side dishes. Shady roadside places like this serve pretty much the same thing you get in the tourist lodges for **about half the price or less**. La Vaca Muca is a particularly nice one. *Info:* On the way out of town towards the cone.

Tropical Fruit Terms

To help you order your *frutas tropicales:*
coco – coconut
guayaba – guava
granadilla – passion fruit
marañón – fruit from the cashew tree, kind of like weird grapes
naranja – orange
piña – pineapple
pipas – green coconuts cut open for the wonderful water (milk) they contain
sandía –watermelon
toronja – grapefruit

BEST EATS IN MONTEVERDE

This is one of the most touristed areas of the country, and that fact is reflected in the dining situation. There are dozens of tourist-oriented restaurants, and most of the hotels have reasonable restaurants. But none of them are at all cheap and most are crowded with—you guessed it—tourists. The service can sometimes be aloof, impersonal, or even downright bad.

The Garden $$$
This is the **best restaurant in town**, although it's a little pricey. The creative menu changes daily and often has a couple of things not on most of the tourist lodge tables. The *ceviche* is usually interesting. The wine list is good, with several levels of Chilean and Spanish wines to choose from. Views out over a cloud-swept valley are nice if you can get a **table at a window**. There is a small, pleasant bar. *Info:* Tel. 257-0766. In Monteverde Lodge.

Dulce Marzo Bakery and Café $$
Located next to Moon Shiva (see below), this is **my favorite place** in town to get my morning pastry, enjoy my fourth or fifth cup of wonderful Costa Rican **coffee**, and **read the newspaper**. Lunch specials, and all the goodies, are made with only the healthiest organic ingredients, of course. Not as crowded as the bakery down the street. The *Gringa* owner makes interesting chocolate gooey things and maintains a pleasant atmosphere. It's quiet. I like it.

Stella's $$
Stella's bakery, on the strip between Santa Elena and Monteverde, bakes **wonderful breads, cakes** etc. On a piece of paper, you check what you want on your sandwich with which kind of bread and everything and they whip it up for you. There is almost always a **long line of tourists** loading up on sandwiches and sticky buns. The service can be snotty, but the food is good. *Info:* Tel. 645-5560. About halfway between Santa Elena and the park entrance.

Moon Shiva $$
They make a good effort to produce healthy, interesting meals and snacks. **Live music at night**. *Info:* Tel. 645-6270.

Treehouse Café $$
Upstairs on the main street in Santa Elena, close to the grocery store, the Treehouse has okay **burgers**, pizzas, beer and **smoothies**. It is aimed directly at tourists but that's okay, because we *are* tourists. You can get a balcony seat and watch the action on the street below: budget travelers staggering under **huge orange backpacks**, ballcap-and-t-shirt-clad families in SUVs with four

kids still red-faced and **screaming fresh from the zip lines,** and behatted twitchers with spotting scopes clutching battered copies of *The Birds of Costa Rica.* I love it.

Chunches, also in Santa Elena, is well known as an interesting bookstore/laundromat/children's **stuff** store. In Costa Rican Spanish, *chunches* means "things" or "stuff."

NORTH PACIFIC COAST

BEST SLEEPS IN THE PAPAGAYO AREA
Four Seasons $$$$
By itself at the very end of Punta Mala, across Bahía Culebra (Snake Bay), opposite Playas del Coco, Playa Hermosa and Playa Panama, the Four Seasons is probably the most luxurious place to stay in the country. The **Arnold Palmer-designed golf course** is one of the top three in the country. There are three swimming pools, two tennis courts (one is a stadium court) and a tropically serene spa. Wireless internet access works over most of the property.

The cheapest rooms here go for over $600 a night, and I fail to see what you get for the extra $200 or so more than anyone else charges. You still have to pay for breakfast ($25), and everything else is an extra charge. Drinks are all over $5 and not any better than you get anywhere else. Service is attentive. The beach is okay, but not spectacular. Still, this *is* a Four Seasons and that means pampering and top-quality service and amenities.

You need a taxi to get anywhere from the hotel. Check on their child policy before booking. *Info:* www.fivestaralliance.com. Tel. 888-5 STAR-11 US.

El Ocotal Beach Resort $$$
Diving central! Ocotal is perched high on a hill overlooking the spectacular bay around Playas del Coco. The view is truly awesome and earns the adjective "panoramic." Be sure you get one of the rooms facing the ocean, or your view will be merely ho-hum.

They have a top-quality **dive operation** right on the property. Fishing for sails and marlin is top-notch just offshore, in season. There always seems to be a troop of howler monkeys in the trees stirring things up. The beach is nice and they have a couple of good bars. The restaurant is nothing that great, but has a wonderful view. Rooms are in motel-style buildings and are quite pleasant with all the goodies, including TVs, AC, phones and safes. *Info:* www.ocotalresort.com. Tel. 670-0321. South of Playas del Coco.

Hotel Flor de Itabo $$$

This is a big-time **fishing lodge** with its own deep-sea fishing fleet, as well as smaller boats for fishing in jungle rivers. Owned by an Italian family, it's been here for 25 years.

The rooms are modern but basic — you come here to fish. Deluxe rooms have air-conditioning, phones, TV, refrigerator and all the usual toiletries. There are also a few apartments with kitchens. The restaurant features Italian cuisine, and they have the obligatory fishermen's bar where tall tales are told. There is a big pool with swim-up bar and a modest beach within walking distance. Prices include free transportation to and from Liberia airport. *Info:* www.flordeitabo.com. Tel. 670-0438, 670-0292. Playas del Coco.

Giardini de Papagayo $$

An all-inclusive resort set on the hills just above Playa Panama, the Giardini has good views from most rooms and is convenient to the beach. The beach is sandy and good for swimming — no rocks. The rooms are in small "villas" with patios and are nicely furnished. There is a **large pool** with some shady areas. Staff can help arrange all types of activities. The **all-inclusive** deals include room, meals, wine and drinks, which is not bad for under $100. *Info:* www.grupopapagayo.com. Tel. 223-1200, 223-7071, 888/790-5264 US. Playa Panama.

El Nakuti $$

Slightly less expensive than the sister property Giardini, El Nakuti also enjoys proximity to the wonderful **Playa Panama**. There is a large pool. Some of the rooms are in freestanding

ld be a good idea to inquire about upgrading to
ecutive suites." Be sure you specify a room with
Info: www.grupopapagayo.com. Tel. 223-1200,
90-5264 US. Playa Panama.

BEST SLEEPS IN THE FLAMINGO AREA
Paradisus Playa Conchal $$$$
Probably the nicest **all-inclusive resort** in Costa Rica, Playa
Conchal has everything you need, and is quietly luxurious. Kids
love the complicated, huge, tropically landscaped pool, one of
the biggest in Latin America with two kiddie pools and two
Jacuzzis. The hamburgers and fries at the pool restaurant are
definitely up to US standards. The eco-recreational **Kid's Club**
keeps them out of your hair, so you can sip umbrella drinks and
play golf. The program is designed to keep them eco-entertained
with two playgrounds, mini climbing wall, mini disco, table
games, movies, eco-recreational team, children's menu, and kid-
size nap areas.

The **Robert Trent Jones** golf course suffers only slightly from
monkeys. The green fee is a mere $125 with cart. There are four
tennis courts, a casino and the obligatory onsite zip line canopy
tour.

The three restaurants are good quality, but nothing like some of
the fine dining spots in the Central Valley. Breakfast buffets have
the required omelet and pancake stations — something for the
whole family.

Battery-powered shuttles roam the property carrying guests to
and fro. The walled property fronts on Playa Conchal, which is
really the only pure white beach in Costa Rica. The finely ground
white shell beach, one of the nicest in the country, is good for
swimming or wandering, and there is **decent snorkeling nearby**.

Although the resort provides everything you need and discour-
ages trips outside the walls, this would be a good base for exploring the other beaches and attractions of the area. Condos with
kitchens are available by the week. You can choose to go with the
all-inclusive deal and eat in the resort, or eat your own cooking and

visit nearby restaurants. There are a couple of nice seafood joints in the nearby village. *Info:* www.paradisusplayaconchal.com. Tel. 654-4123. Brasilito.

Flamingo Beach Resort $$
Playa Flamingo is directly in front of this place, so you can enjoy the **beach activities** and easily slip back to your room to freshen up. Ocean-view suites are the preferred rooms, as they are quieter than the poolside rooms. You can go for their all-inclusive rate of $140 for two, which includes meals and **lots of booze.** The wonderful restaurant **Marie's** is just across the street. Of course there is a central pool with swim-up bar and lighted tennis courts. There are three restaurants with room service and two bars.

Marina Maybe

The **Flamingo Marina Resort,** home to numerous fishing tournaments, is sadly run-down. The **condos** are much nicer than the regular hotel rooms, but boost the cost into the $$$ range.

I have had reports of overbooking, so be sure to confirm well in advance and call or fax again a night or two before arriving. Check their web site or call for specials. *Info:* www.resortflamingobeach.com. Tel. 654-4444, 888/500-9090 US. Playa Flamingo.

BEST SLEEPS IN THE TAMARINDO AREA
Hotel El Jardín del Edén $$$
Perched on the hill just behind town, the Edén boasts a panoramic vista of Tamarindo Bay, probably the **best view** of all the local hotels. The new French owners have made extensive upgrades to the property.

The 34 rooms are in five villas, and are individually isolated and reasonably private. All the rooms have AC, ceiling fans, TVs, phones, safes, hair dryers and balconies or patios. There are also two apartments with kitchens.

The pool and Jacuzzi are lovely, surrounded by green vegetation, with tropical umbrella drink "poolside services." The restaurant has wonderful **Italian food** and great views. It's a walk into town or to the beach, which is not so bad. The walk back up the hill however, is something to consider. *Info:* www.jardindeleden.com. Tel. 653-0137.

Hotel Capitán Suizo $$$

Everyone loves this place. Right by one of the best parts of the beach, it is a little out of town, but that's not a bad thing. It is one of the more luxurious properties in Tamarindo. Pool, restaurant and bar are pleasant and only a few steps from the beach. It is a member of Small Distinctive Hotels of Costa Rica.

The 22 rooms and eight bungalows are very cheerful, with stone floors and whimsical colors on the walls. Amenities include phones, safes and refrigerators. Sliding glass doors open onto patios or balconies. If you like sleeping with a cool tropical breeze, ask for one of the rooms on the upper floor. *Info:* www.hotelcapitansuizo.com. Tel. 653-0075.

Villa Alegre $$$

One of the nicest B&Bs I have visited, Villa Alegre is well run by Barry and Suzye Lawson. It's just above the beach, Playa Langosta, with **good surfing right in front**. The wonderful sound of surf fills the air. You can walk to town along the beach. The owners are very friendly and are glad to help you find your way around. Barry is an avid golfer and knows all the pros in the area.

All the rooms are individually air-conditioned and have safes. A couple of fluffy dogs are available if needed. You are allowed to raid the refrigerator at night. There is a nice pool. This is one of the most pleasant of the few actual beachfront lodgings in Tamarindo. Villa Alegre is **one of my favorite places to stay**. *Info:* www.villaalegrecostarica.com. Tel. 653-0270.

Hotel y Villas Cala Luna $$$

The villas at Cala Luna are **simply fantastic**. I love the stucco Pacific Rim architecture. The basic rooms are okay, but the villas with their **private plunge pools**, kitchens, etc. are isolated, quiet and special. Honeymooners love the privacy. They are nicely decorated and well furnished. They come with full kitchens, laundry and everything you need to escape. The restaurant serves fresh seafood, pasta and steaks, but I find more interesting places to eat nearby. It is very nice but a little pricey for a place that's not directly on the beach (the beach is across the street and down a path). *Info:* www.calaluna.com. Tel. 653-0214.

Barceló Playa Langosta $$$

This downmarket hotel is directly on one of the best surf beaches around, Playa Langosta, right in front of the best break, and is therefore jam-packed with **surfers**. The tiki bar by the pool **blares loud music** all day and much of the night. This might just be your thing. It is very much an old motel-style building. *Info:* www.barcelo.com. Tel. 653-0363, 220-2034, 800/227-2356 US.

BEST SLEEPS SOUTH OF TAMARINDO
Hacienda Pinilla $$$$

Hacienda Pinilla is a very large (4,500 acres) luxury residential development where you can purchase homes, beach villas and condos, or simply stay in opulence and enjoy the **Mike Young-designed golf course**. The luxurious, expensive resort has an abundance of everything that appeals to the upmarket traveler.

Amenities include three miles of coastline, extensive stables and riding facilities, lighted **tennis courts**, and on and on. The **Posada del Sol** hotel, beach houses and **Casa Golf Suites** offer a variety of top quality options. They have interesting specials that can make Pinilla a reasonably priced option for luxury accommodations in the area.

The list of activities is endless. The staff arranges all manner of trips to local attractions and adventures. In spite of the snobby atmosphere, Pinilla is the sponsor of the annual Costa Rica-wide **Pinilla Classic National Surfing Championships**. Even hardcore twitchers won't be disappointed with over 300 species of birds to choose from. *Info:* www.haciendapinilla.com. Tel. 680-7060.

Hotel Punta Islita $$$$

A member of the Small Luxury Hotels of the World group, Punta Islita is **one of the best hotels in the country**. The views out to the Pacific from the rooms and from the infinity pool are spectacular.

The beach is a short walk and is a **good swimming beach**. There is another pool with a bar by the beach, right at the edge of the sand.

Service is almost over the top—arriving guests are greeted with hot towels and refreshing fruit drinks. The cabinas are immaculate, luxurious and romantic with hammocks just big enough for two and **very private plunge pools** surrounded by exotic tropical vegetation with views out over the Pacific, also just big enough for two. This is a very good choice for a wedding venue. The hotel is, deservedly, very popular with honeymooners. It is isolated and quiet.

The restaurant is one of the best on the coast, heavy with seafood and with a good wine list, mostly Spanish and Chilean. The cabinas are romantic. In the evenings, the restaurant is thick with honeymooners mooning over their tables at each other with cow eyes.

The trip to the hotel by road is interesting. Make sure you call ahead to check on the tides, as a couple of the rivers you'll have to cross can get high. In the green season, portions of the road are almost impassable. They have **their own airport** with a good road to the hotel, so you can always get there. Call ahead. *Info:* www.hotelpuntaislita.com. Tel. 231-6122, 290-4259.

Guanamar $$
With 40 air-conditioned rooms and suites with all the trimmings, Guanamar is a **fishing-oriented** resort. It is a little worn but otherwise comfortable. The rooms all have AC, safes, TVs and phones. Restaurant, bar and pool are nice with great views out to sea. Fish on the menu comes from local fishermen.

This is one of the top fishing tournament locations in the country. The best fishing grounds are not very far offshore, so fishing time is maximized in this area. It is not unusual to hook 25 or 30 sailfish and a couple of marlin in one day. Guanamar is the place to make this kind of fishing action happen. *Info:* www.hotelguanamar.com. Tel. 656-0054.

BEST SLEEPS IN TAMBOR, MONTEZUMA, MALPAÍS

Hotel Flor Blanca $$$$

With only ten separate stucco and tile villas, the Flor Blanca is one of the quietest, **most luxurious** and interesting places to stay in Costa Rica. Although the original developers have left the scene, the hotel continues to offer hip, upscale travelers deluxe beachfront digs. At $400 a night, one expects only the best linens, furniture and decorations. There's a New Age, Pac Rim atmosphere. Facilities include a two-level pool with waterfall, music room with **piano**, art studio, yoga/pilates studio, a **dojo for karate and yoga,** and a big Tai-chi scene.

The hotel is located in Santa Teresa on the dirt road leading north from Malpaís. The **surfing** in the area is legendary.

Their literature states that no children under the age of 13 are allowed, but their website has pictures of babies enjoying the pool with mummy. Maybe they make exceptions if you are the Kennedys, who are rumored to rent the whole place for weeks at a time.

I have heard reports that the level of service has deteriorated with the new owners. Some staff may have been hired for surfing

Avoid Bahía Luminosa

I no longer recommend the Hotel Bahía Luminosa. It used to be a beautiful property, but has become sadly run-down in the last few years.

ability and coolness rather than service attitude and hospitality experience. *Info:* www.florblanca.com. Tel. 640-0232.

Tambor Tropical $$$

The rooms are all large, beautiful suites with **imaginative and detailed woodwork,** full kitchens and all the goodies. The shady grounds front on the beach, but are also right in the village, so the beach is a little on the busy side and the hotel itself gets **noisy.** Most rooms face the bar and pool, which can be a problem, as the bar can get interesting (loud) as the night wears on. There are plenty of shady hammocks. No kids. *Info:* www.tambortropical.com. Tel. 365-2872, 866/890-2537 US.

Hotel Tango Mar $$$

This is a luxurious 150-acre resort with a **nine-hole golf course** fronting right on one of the most visually **spectacular beaches** in the country. The Belgian owners have recently remodeled all the rooms and public spaces. The villas are on a hill above the beach and have fantastic views out towards the Pacific. The Cristóbal restaurant features (of course) seafood, and is quite good.

The beach is amazing, with awesome surf and photogenic waterfalls. The TV show *Temptation Island* was filmed here. On-site are a pool and tennis courts (bring your own racket). There's not much else in the area, but Tambor, Montezuma and Mal País are a short drive away. Great! *Info:* www.tangomar.com. Tel. 683-0001.

El Sano Banano / Ylang Ylang Beach Resort $$$
El Sano Banano Village Hotel (careful: there is a Sano Banano Hotel in Puntarenas that is not the same place) offers 12 basic but comfortable air-conditioned rooms above the restaurant of the same name, which has long been a favorite in Montezuma.

The same outfit operates the much more interesting Ylang Ylang Beach Resort, which is **on the beach** about 15 minutes from the village. There is no road to the hotel — you have to walk (the staff will bring your luggage). All by itself amid miles of unspoiled jungle, the resort features eight little cabins, some with outdoor garden showers, a waterfall pool and an outdoor restaurant — *muy romantico* by candlelight at night. This might be the secluded paradise we have all been looking for! *Info:* www.elbanano.com. Tel. 642-0636.

BEST EATS IN THE FLAMINGO AREA
Camarón Dorado $$$
Local sport-fishing captain Jorge Segueira runs the **best place to eat** for miles around in Brasilito. It's usually packed. Tourists love the simply prepared and well-presented **seafood**, right on the beach with the breeze blowing through. It's a little pricey but worth a splurge. Very romantic. *Info:* Tel. 654-4028.

Costa Rican Riviera

The Nicoya Peninsula and the little bit of coast to the north is experiencing a boom in tourist traffic and development. Huge resort hotel projects are underway or are being planned. With the airport in Liberia now handling 15 to 20 flights from North America daily, eating and sleeping options are quite varied and growing. In most areas, the best eating is at the restaurants of the lodges and hotels. A few towns like Tamarindo are big enough to offer a choice of interesting restaurants. Eating roast fish and drinking beer in thatched huts by the water is definitely on.

Marie's Restaurant $$
Near the Hotel Playa Flamingo, Marie's has no particular view or anything, but it does have good food and a nice atmosphere. **Grand fish sandwiches**. The juice drips off your elbow as you bite into them. *Info:* Tel. 654-4136.

BEST EATS IN THE TAMARINDO AREA
Lazy Wave $$$
I can't get enough of the **Pacific Rim fusion** at the Lazy Wave. It is a little off the street near the Hotel Pasatiempo. You have to kind of bump through the parking lot to get to it. Even though it's not cheap, it's always packed. The beer is served in glasses with ice but aside from this **quaint custom**, all the food is top-notch. Try to get a stool by the kitchen so you can see the cooks at work. **Chalkboard specials** are the deal. Seafood, seafood, seafood. *Info:* Tel. 653-0737.

Gecko's $$
In the Iguana Surf Shop, Gecko's does a good job, with great **seafood** for breakfast, lunch and dinner. You can eat great hunks of mahi and tuna.

BEST EATS IN TAMBOR, MONTEZUMA, MALPAÍS
Pancho's $$$
On the water at the edge of Tambor, over by the fishermen's dock and the yacht club, is Pancho's, with some of the **freshest seafood** you'll ever find. It's **not cheap** ($45 for a lobster!) after being inundated by the big-spending production staff of the TV show

Temptation Island for months of shooting. The service is good. The dogs are friendly but usually asleep.

Sano Banano $$
Right in the middle of Montezuma is the popular Sano Banano, famous for **banana pancakes** and *pargo entero*. You have to eat here at least once. Try to get a seat with a view of the street action, such as it is. They show dubious movies after dinner. *Info:* Tel. 642-0638.

CENTRAL PACIFIC COAST

BEST SLEEPS IN JACÓ
Los Sueños Marriott Ocean and Golf Resort $$$$
Probably **the snazziest lodging in the area**, Los Sueños seems to have it all. Once you are in the gates of this US-style development you'd never know if you were in Florida, California, or wherever. A Ted Robinson-designed **golf course** sets the tone for the whole place. The huge **marina** with its big-buck yachts is the largest in Central America, and is home to various fishing tournaments and some of the best captains in Costa Rica. It hosts large yachts for celebrities such as George Strait.

This is a luxury hotel with six restaurants, casino, bars, deluxe rooms and suites and business-service amenities. The best of their restaurants, **La Vista**, is the finest on the coast. Their **seafood buffet** with lobster is legendary. The only drawback is the beach. It is dirty gravel and simply not very appealing. The pool is elaborate and almost makes up for the lousy beach. *Info:* www.lossuenosresort.com. Tel. 637-8886, 866/865-9759 US. Playa Herradura, just north of Jacó.

Villas Caletas $$$$
Perched on a hill with **a breathtaking view of the sea and sky**, Villas Caletas is another very good option for the luxury traveler. It's close to Jacó, with all the dubious pleasures of that beach town, but secluded and quiet. **Wedding parties and honey-**

mooners make up a significant part of their clientele. It is a member of Small Distinctive Hotels of Costa Rica.

This resort is aimed squarely at upmarket, jaded travelers. There are only 31 rooms, out of which 14 are stand-alone villas and 11 are suites. The elaborate décor is in an Italianate Art Deco style. Every luxury amenity is here, including nice touches such as bathrobes, umbrellas and little bottles of designer goo in the bathrooms.

There are two restaurants and a bar. French-influenced cuisine is served in the formal El Mirador, or outdoors in a faux Greek amphitheatre overlooking the ocean. *Info:* www.hotelvillacaletas.com. Tel. 637-0505.

Rowdy Beach Town

If the nightlife and beach-town scene keep you awake at night, you might want to consider staying outside Jacó and coming into town only when you need a bar, restaurant, t-shirt shop, or just feel like looking at the girls on the beach. All of the lodging in town, except for the Hotel Club del Mar, is at the **lower end of the quality scale**. However, it's a young town, and most visitors come specifically to be close to the loud and rowdy beach town scene (in contrast to the advice I give here). Just realize that there are options if you are looking for a more luxurious and comfortable place to stay in the area.

Hotel Club Del Mar $$$
This is by far the best of the hotels in Jacó. It is at the extreme south end of town right on the beach, out of the hurly-burly. It is really the only hotel I can recommend in Jacó, and I recommend it wholeheartedly. If you are looking for **a palm-shaded beach vacation** with some restaurants and shopping nearby, this is the place. I like Jacó but find the choice of lodging to be dismal. Hotel Club Del Mar lets you enjoy the funky beach town while wallowing in luxury nearby.

There are a few hotel-style rooms, but the best ones are the freestanding condos they rent, most of which have two bedrooms and come completely furnished with everything you need, including full kitchens and **washer/dryers**. The beds are king-size. The AC is ice cold. They have TVs with cable, phones, too many towels and all the expected luxury goodies. A couple of the rooms experience some noise from trucks with their Jake brakes coming down the hill, so request one close to the beach.

Everything is right in the palm trees at the top of the beach. You can surf in front of the rooms just past the pool. **Surf and boogie boards** are available at the front desk. Wireless internet is available in the lobby and some of the rooms.

The restaurant may seem a little expensive, but they serve good food and are a little cleaner and nicer than the others in town. They usually have some mid-quality combo or solo artist entertaining in the bar/restaurant in the evenings. *Info:* www.clubdelmarcostarica.com. Tel. 634-3194, 866/978-5669 US.

BEST SLEEPS IN MANUEL ANTONIO
Some of the great Manuel Antonio hotels from the past, such as the **Mariposa,** have faded in glory. However, the **Parador** is still wonderful and the exclusive **La Mansión** has been proclaimed to be the overall best hotel in Costa Rica. It is. The new and extremely upscale, Miami Beach-ish **Gaia** sets a new level of luxury for Manuel Antonio.

El Parador $$$$
Waaay up on a hill overlooking both of the beautiful bays around Manuel Antonio, El Parador is one of the nicest two or three properties in the area. The atmosphere is **Old Spain** with suits of armor, dark wood paneling and heavy Castilian furniture. The restaurant and bar are top-notch. Don't miss grilled lobster night. They have a good selection of Spanish wines with interesting bottles in several price categories. Security is tight and service excellent. The owners live on the property and keep an eagle eye on the operations. Facilities include **tennis courts**, spa services, **infinity swimming pool**, and special event rooms. *Info:* www.hotelparador.com. Tel. 777-1414.

La Mansión $$$$
Luxury travel boffins have pronounced La Mansión to be **the best hotel in Costa Rica**, and few can dispute the claim. If you can get

in, you are **pampered and spoiled** with a staff ratio of
1 to 1. It's quiet and seems small. International **celeb...**
diplomats lease the whole place for themselves and their retinues
from time to time. There's plenty of room for bodyguards and
nannies.

Although it can be a little hard to get a reservation during the high
season, you should definitely call or e-mail to see if there are any
specials available. Sometimes you can get a nice room here for a
special price and live in luxury for a few days. It is certainly
intimate enough to make a wonderful honeymoon spot. You can
easily pop in for a visit to the foggy Bat Cave bar. They have a
good choice of wines by the glass.

The restaurant is outstanding. The wines are from Harry's own
wine cellar. The views over the beaches and bays to the Pacific
are stupendous. Monkeys and sloths visit the pool. The hippest
beach in town is nearby. *Info:* www.lamansioninn.com. Tel. 777-
3489, 777-5011.

Gaia Hotel and Reserve $$$$
Gaia is a new, very contemporary, **Miami Beach-style** addition
to the scene, all stark white and stainless steel, with **square toilets**
and flat-screen TVs. Like all the other hotels in town, it is perched
on a hill with **a helluva view**. Currently, this is the snazziest hotel
in Costa Rica and they're still working on it. The restaurant is
great but very pricey. The wine list is extensive but also very
pricey. Go for it. *Info:* www.gaiahr.com. Tel. 777-2239, 800/226-
2515 US.

Hotel Si Como No Resort $$$
Even though the resort is sort of jam-packed together, everybody
likes Si Como No. It is getting a little long in the tooth, but still
retains its **Disneyesque** charm. It is like a jungly movie set, with
stair rails shaped like snakes. The owner was a set designer at the
Disney studios and brought his sense of style to the design of the
hotel. They have their own movie theater with Hollywood specials every night. It's set on a hillside above the ocean, so you need
to take a hotel shuttle or taxi to get to the beach. There are two
pools, one for adults only next to the restaurant. A fading popular

honeymoon destination, it maintains its tropical charm. *Info:* www.sicomono.com. Tel. 777-0777.

Villas Makanda $$$

Bungalowish rooms overlook the bay, with hammocks and lounges. The rooms are very tropical, open-air with **romantic mosquito nets** and ceiling fans. Breakfast is served in your room or on the balcony, but be careful, the **monkeys** will snatch food from your tray if you are not watching. There is a nice beach a couple of hundred steps down the hill. Very charming. Great for weddings and honeymoons. This is a good choice in Manuel Antonio. *Info:* www.makanda.com. Tel. 777-0442.

BEST SLEEPS IN THE CHIRRIPÓ REGION
Rió Chirripó Retreat $$

This pleasant lodge sits above the Chirripó River, in a 12-acre tract of beautiful forest. The eight guest rooms each have a bathroom and a private balcony. There are also three "luxury tent platforms" and a very nice pool down by the river. The owners, a friendly American couple, serve up gourmet vegetarian fare, and host a variety of **spiritual and health-conscious events**, including ortho-bionomy, yoga and watsu. The lovely setting, friendly staff and air of spirituality make this a very special place.

San Gerardo de Rivas is the gateway for hikes on Costa Rica's highest mountain, Cerro de Chirripó. Up here, the vegetation is tropical, but the climate is cool and spring-like year-round. Air conditioning is simply not necessary.

There are a couple of other decent lodges in San Gerardo de Rivas, but some are only open during the winter months. There are also a few cheap hotels, with restaurants, of varying levels of cleanliness. *Info:* www.riochirripo.com. Tel. 364-9527, 858-9885. San Gerardo de Rivas.

Trogon Lodge $$

The Trogon Lodge is probably the most **beautiful tropical lodge** I have seen anywhere. It is set in the bottom of a steep valley near the headwaters of the Rió Savegre and surrounded by acres and acres of highly manicured landscaping with thousands of flowers and exotic shrubs. Hummingbirds, **quetzals**, and even trogons flit about. Trout ponds in front of and around the lodge provide wonderful eating in the lodge restaurant.

Visitors enjoy walks and a zip line through the nearby cloud forest. The lodge maintains a modest horse stable. This is one of the most desired destinations for **birders** in the world. The food is good and the rooms are comfortable.

The lodge is waaay up in the mountains and it gets quite chilly. The rooms have heaters. You'll need a jacket. This would be a good overnight (or more) stopping point when driving from San José to the southern Pacific area. The same company operates the beachfront Mawamba Lodge in Tortuguero. *Info:* www.grupomawamba.com/ trogonlodge. Tel. 293-8181. San Gerardo de Dota, near Cerro de la Muerte.

BEST EATS IN JACÓ
Pacific Bistro $$$
Right on the strip, the Pacific serves dinner only. **California fusion**: Thai/local seafood/LA/San Francisco/Tokyo sauce. I suggest calling ahead to reserve a table near the street. The **friendly Gringo** owner keeps the hustlers off. The food is good. Tuna comes in huge chunks. *Info:* Tel. 643-3771.

Colonial $$$
The Colonial is a regular old tourist restaurant on the strip with a **nice bar** and comfortable seats with a view of the action. The food is a little better than most of the other, similar-looking places nearby. My companion liked the **snook with mango sauce**. I do, liked the snapper. I had to shoo off annoying bead salesmen twice during our meal. No big deal. *Info:* Tel. 653-3332.

Pancho Villa's $$$
This Mexican eatery serves enchiladas and tacos, steaks and lobster and a castle of shrimp, for $6 to $20. It's fair. Whatever you **don't go upstairs**. It's a nightclub,

Pass On The Poseidon

Pass on the Poseidon restaurant. While it is recommended by all the local hotels, I find it to be noisy, not so clean, and beset by hustlers.

bad scene, with bimbos hustling drinks, etc. but the restaurant is okay. On the strip.

Marisquería el Hicaco $$$

This open-air place right by the beach is a fine spot to **gobble big piles of reasonably priced seafood**. Wednesday **lobster** night is famous. Some of the tables have a view of the beach action. The beer is cold but the wine list is basic. It's not a wine kind of place.

El Bohío $$

El Bohío is a **crummy little beach bar** and restaurant with a view of the beach where all sorts of surfing and skimpy bathing suit strutting is going on, right in front. You can lean on the rail sipping a beer on ice, taking in the scene while **stuffing your face** with whole fish, regular old bar-food sandwiches, shrimp, etc. It's a happenin' spot and gets crowded. **I love it.**

BEST EATS IN MANUEL ANTONIO/QUEPOS
Jacques Cousteau Dining Room $$$$

If you want an elegant, truly **gourmet-quality** meal in a small, quiet, **romantic setting** and you are willing to pay for it, the Jacques Cousteau Dining Room at La Mansión Inn is a good choice. Call a couple of days before you would like to dine to discuss your meal - reservations are essential. There are just a few tables.

The **wonderful wine list** is heavy on Argentinean and Chilean reds personally selected by the owner on his travels. Few realize that the restaurant will accept guests not staying at the hotel. Expect the best. *Info:* Tel. 777-3489, 777-5011. In the hotel La Mansión.

Claro Que Seafood $$$

This pleasant seafood restaurant has **some of the nicest food in town**. It's a little upscale, and the honeymooners staying in the Hotel Si Como No find it to be romantic. Be sure to call for a reservation. *Info:* Tel. 777-0777. In the Hotel Si Como No.

Karola's $$$

In spite of nearby construction, Karola's maintains its air of tropical, **international tiki-hut** beach bar, even though it's not particularly close to any beach or anything. The food includes ribs, Mexican dishes, huge shrimp, roasted garlic, and "the freshest tuna anywhere." The margaritas are strong. So is the garlic. *Info:* Tel. 777-1557. Just before the turn to the Mariposa.

El Gran Escape $$$
One of the most famous places in Quepos, El Gran Escape is a nice fishermen's bar with good sandwiches and seafood grills—a very good deal. They serve North American food in a large room with lamps dangling from the ceiling and posters decorating the walls. Portions are very large. If you like palm hearts, the palm heart salad here could founder you. Pizza, huge fish sandwiches, and burgers—it's all good. I like the place a lot. Breakfast or a full meal can cost under $10. Wine is available but large beers and larger rum and tequila drinks are popular here. No pretense: just good food. This is **the best spot in Quepos**. *Info:* Tel. 777-0395. On the main street in Quepos.

SOUTH PACIFIC COAST

BEST SLEEPS IN DRAKE BAY
La Paloma Lodge $$$
Here you'll find luxury food and lodgings with an emphasis on **scuba diving**. You are right in the jungle but with a fantastic view out to sea. Rooms are tropical, with the breeze blowing through. The lodge is high atop a hill, with incredible views out to Caño Island. Bring your binoculars to spot whales, dolphins and a host of seabirds.

The rooms and open-air "ranchos" have beautiful wood décor, ceiling fans and balconies with splendid views. Prevailing westerly winds keep things reasonably cool year-round.

The food is one of the most memorable things about La Paloma. Fresh fruit, local seafood and organic produce are the basis for interesting meals served in the open-air dining room/lounge. **Cheeky monkeys** will help themselves to the breakfast buffet if you don't watch out. Scrabble tournaments rage for months at a time. *Info:* www.lapalomalodge.com. Tel. 293-7502.

Aguila de Osa $$$

Aguila de Osa is run by two wonderful tropical characters. Owner Bradd Johnson and Manager Pedro Garro are personable and interested in making sure their guests have a good time enjoying the nearby Corcovado National Park, fishing, diving or observing dolphins.

The Aguila has the best **sport-fishing** operation in the area and is well equipped for divers. The food is tremendous, the wine flows freely and the CD selection behind the bar is awesome.

The rooms are not luxurious, but are fairly comfortable, and most have great views. Coffee is brought to your door in the morning in a thermos. You need to get it quickly, before the monkeys do. Monkeys cranked up on caffeine are not a pretty sight. **I love this place**. *Info:* www.aguiladeosainn.com. Tel. 296-2190, 866/924-8452 US.

Drake Bay Lodges

There are several lodges clustered around a small inlet, several of them upscale. Corcovado National Park is close, so exploration activities occupy most visitors. Electricity can be unreliable. Fishing and diving are wonderful. Whales, dolphins and crocs populate the waters. Access is by a barely passable dirt road, by air or by boat.

BEST SLEEPS IN CORCOVADO PARK

Corcovado Lodge Tent Camp $$

Located right at the edge of **Corcovado National Park** near Carate, the tent camp is without a doubt the best and most comfortable way to enjoy **the most remote and unspoiled area of Costa Rica**. And I do mean remote — you walk on the beach for about a mile to get to the lodge (your luggage rides comfortably in a donkey cart).

You can't get any further out into the jungle without actually camping. In spite of the word "tent" in the name, it is extremely comfortable. The tents are set up over wooden platforms, and each has two beds and a nightstand inside. That's it. Bathrooms are nearby.

The food is served communally and is definitely wonderful. Shrimp, fish, steaks and local produce are well prepared and plentiful. One night when shrimp was for dinner, there were large platters with dozens and dozens of great big shrimp—more than we could eat! The **piña coladas** are superb.

I suppose the best thing about the lodge is that it is right next to the park. The Osa is the least disturbed area of the country and is astoundingly rich in wildlife. If you want to see wildlife, there are no better places to do it. Trails into the park start just outside the property. A long walk along the beach will almost certainly yield numerous animal sightings. Twitchers add significantly to their life lists from a platform set up by the lodge high in the forest canopy.

The lodge is just above the high-tide line in the palm trees above one of the most beautiful beaches I have seen anywhere. **Scarlet macaws** by the dozen hang around making a racket. Howler monkeys add to the noise. The sound of the surf never leaves you—the roar lulls you to sleep. You never want to leave. *Info:* www.costaricaexpeditions.com. Tel. 257-0766.

BEST SLEEPS IN PUERTO JIMÉNEZ
Lapa Ríos $$$$
Lapa Ríos is without doubt **the most luxurious eco-lodge in the country**. It's one of only two hotels in the country to earn a perfect sustainable tourism score of five green leaves from the Costa Rican Tourist Board. The food is superb, the rooms are unique and the location is stunning. I saw three different types of monkeys from my balcony in two days. **Toucans** chattered up a storm.

They only have 16 rooms, which are all separate luxurious bungalows. You follow a long wooden walkway through the jungle to get to your rooms. Keep the door to the deck shⁱ are not paying attention, or the **monkeys** may come in a themselves to whatever seems interesting.

it is more formal than in other nearby lodges, with es and a menu with selections. Banana pancakes t.

All the usual tours and activities can be arranged, including a walk through the forest examining medicinal herbs led by a local *brujo* (witch) or medicine man, who claims to be part shaman and part showman. *Info:* www.laparios.com. Tel. 735-5130, 735-5281.

Iguana Lodge $$$

This super-friendly lodge is on the deserted **Plantares Beach**, which is great for surfing, boogie boarding and long walks. Dogs are provided for beach walks if requested. The unique tropical-style rooms are luxurious, with good mattresses, fluffy pillows and excellent reading lights. Some of the showers are actually in a walled garden outside the rooms. If you like, your room can be provided with a cat.

The food is excellent (they have the best chef in Osa) and owners Toby and Lauren Cleaver keep the wine and good conversation flowing. You really have the feeling you are staying in a guest cottage at their home. This is **one of my very favorite lodges in Costa Rica**.

The location is convenient to Corcovado National Park and Puerto Jiménez. The Cleavers know all the best fishing captains and tour guides and can set you up with all the usual activities. *Info:* www.iguanalodge.com. Tel. 829-5865.

Crocodile Bay Lodge $$$

Crocodile Bay is **the best-run fishing lodge in the country**. It is usually packed with Gringos anxious to haul in sailfish, marlin, roosterfish, tuna, mahi and snapper. The all-inclusive packages are slightly more expensive than some of the other lodges, but you get what you pay for. Service for fishing activities and the hotel/restaurant is tops.

The rooms are the nicest of any fishing lodge I have visited. Large and air-conditioned, with two queen-size beds, they have everything, including coffee makers, safes and racks to store your fishing poles.

The food is superb, with groaning buffets of seafood and steaks. US-style specials and local Tico-style rice and bean dishes compete for your attention. When they grill steaks you can choose between filet, T-bone and NY strip, or settle for a huge pork chop or Cajun chicken.

The **booze flows freely** (literally) at the bar and the drinks are great. If you feel your daiquiri isn't strong enough, just say so and the bartender will start pouring it full of rum until you tell him to stop.

Fishing Director Todd Staley runs the fishing side of things with humor and efficiency. He has his eye on everything. The **boats and tackle are top-notch** and all the guides speak English. The emphasis is definitely on fishing. Management knows what their guests come for, and make sure everyone gets the type of fishing experience they want. When I arrived mid-morning with my fishing buddy, we were settled in our room and out on the water fishing within 10 minutes of our arrival.

There is an enormous **new and luxurious spa** with all the latest services. The gift shop, although on the overpriced side, is the best in the area by far.

If you count the cost of lodging, flying into the area, food and fishing, the high price starts to make sense. If you do all of this on your own, and hire independent local captains, you will probably spend more money and have less time for fishing. *Info:* www.crocodilebay.com. Tel. 735-5631, 800/733-1115 US.

BEST SLEEPS IN THE GOLFITO AREA
Esquinas Rainforest Lodge $$$
If you are serious about **eco-adventuring** and like to be out in the middle of nowhere with experienced naturalists to talk to, Esquinas may be for you. It is only a few miles from Golfito and a mile or two off the Pan American Highway, but it's in the middle of primary and secondary rain forest, with not much else

around. An Austrian group donated land for the lodge and the nearby **Gamba Biological Research Station.**

The food in the restaurant is good. The pool is really amazing. A mountain stream runs right through it (cold!) and it is crystal clear and has *no* chemicals. There is a caiman pond on the lodge grounds but watch out! Some of the caimans are actually plastic! The rooms are basic but comfortable. If you have the oomph, there is a long hike from the lodge over the mountain to the Golfo Dulce. *Info:* www.esquinaslodge.com. Tel. 775-0140. Just outside Golfito.

BEST SLEEPS IN ZANCUDO
Roy's Zancudo Lodge $$$

Roy Ventura, the father of Costa Rican sport fishing, has been running his world-famous fishing lodge for over 25 years. This is a place for **serious anglers**. The rooms are air-conditioned, with all the amenities you would expect in a nice hotel anywhere, including TVs and phones.

The restaurant serves up wonderful seafood (snook, shrimp, tuna) and killer desserts. Roy's is right on the beach. **Zancudo Beach** is long and wide with world-class surfing nearby. There is almost nothing else going on in Zancudo except for a couple of *pulperías* and a bar or two.

One of the nicest things about staying with Roy is Roy. He is full of the most astounding fishing stories you will ever hear. His boats and equipment are top-quality and kept up-to-date. The lodge location is good for getting to the billfishing grounds. It is particularly well located for roosterfish.

I've stayed in most of the fishing lodges in Costa Rica and feel there is little real quality difference between them. When I am at other lodges, the talk always gets around to gossiping about the various lodges I've stayed at, their owners and staff. Everyone in the country has good things to say about Roy. Everyone likes him. You will catch fish at any of the lodges, but **only Roy's Zancudo has Roy Ventura**. *Info:* www.royszancudolodge.com. Tel. 776-0008, 877/529-6980 US.

BEST EATS IN PUERTO JIMÉNEZ

Head to any of the hotels and jungle lodges in this section for the best dining along the South Pacific coast. There are a couple of decent restaurants I'd recommend is in **Puerto Jiménez**, below:

Buena Esperanza $$

Also called **Martina's**, Buena Esperanza is a few miles outside town on the left, on the road towards **Matapalo**. It's really the only place to get a beer for many a mile, and serves great sandwiches and special meals. If you want a feast you will need to ask the interesting German owner, Martina, in advance. This is a great local hangout and a good stop (in fact, the only one) for a cold drink on the way to **Corcovado**.

Skip Juanita's Beer Garden

Make sure you skip **Juanita's Beer Garden**, often recommended to tourists. Little care is taken with the sort-of-Mexican food, and dishes are often served cold. They never had beer or any other alcoholic beverage when I visited, and there is certainly no garden, let alone a "beer garden." As far as I can tell, the Chinese cook is incapable of preparing palatable Mexican food. I've given the place several chances but gave up.

Restaurante Carolina $

Right about where the bus lets out, open to the street, Carolina's is the hangout of preference for the moment, with fish, and meat *casados* for $4 or less. The food is fine and cheap. Their fruit smoothies are wonderful but somehow don't last long enough.

12. BEST ACTIVITIES

SHOPPING

Champion shoppers agree that Costa Rica suffers in comparison to neighboring countries when it comes to good local handcrafts, but there are a few gems to be found. Tourist shops selling artsy stuff are plentiful, but many of the craft items come from Mexico or Guatemala. Toucans made from every material known to man seem to be the most common tourist trinket, followed closely by turtles made from the same stuff.

Coffee and rum make good gifts for the folks back home. Both are best purchased in a local grocery store. The duty-free shop at the airport is not any cheaper. Prices in tourist shops around the country are usually higher.

San José
The Central Market is not really aimed at tourists and t-shirts, but in Barrio Tournón, you'll find **El Centro Commercial del Pueblo,**

where there are all sorts of tourist-oriented shops, restaurants and evening folklore shows. I find the area insufferable, but it's all about tourists in buses.

Sarchí
An hour or so outside San José is the crafts-oriented town of **Sarchí**. Famous for its gaudily-painted ox carts, there are dozens of small shops selling the usual tourist stuff: toucans, turtles and t-shirts.

Guaitíl
Guaitíl, on the Nicoya Peninsula, is one of the few really interesting shopping opportunities in the country. The town is close to clay deposits and has grown up over the years into a pottery center. The local designs are quite attractive. You can watch the potters at work. Some of the stores can arrange for shipping back to the US. The majority of the potteries are run by women.

Jacó
Get your t-shirts and other tourist supplies on the strip in Jacó. There are dozens of shops selling the usual fridge magnets, stickers and toucans. They are all pretty much the same. A lot of the stuff is made in Mexico or Guatemala.

Just outside Jacó, about a mile south of town on the left, is a woodcarving shop, where a very nice geezer named **Eugenio** makes wonderful furniture out of exotic woods. He doesn't have a fancy showroom or anything, but there are always lots of interesting works in progress lying about.

Manuel Antonio
Very little of interest is available in the tourist shops in Manuel Antonio. At the end of the main road near the park entrance are dozens of stalls selling the usual t-shirts, wraps, plastic toucans, and such.

NIGHTLIFE & ENTERTAINMENT

San José
Because of the unsafe nature of the streets at night, nightlife in San José is perhaps best limited to excursions to the **Jazz Café** (Tel. 253-8933) in San Pedro, the student part of town. San José is a world-famous famous nightlife destination, but most of the fame is based on gambling at the **Horseshoe**, or pursuing the dubious pleasures of ladies of the night at the **Blue Marlin Bar** (Tel. 257-7800). Otherwise it would be best to make an early night of it. Get up early and go on a bird walk.

Jacó

Jacó has more happening after dark than any other beach town in Costa Rica. Entertainment options run from regular old bars to discos, Latin dance emporiums, drum-and-bass places, whorehouses, "nightclubs" and sports bars. You might like **Disco La Central** (Tel. 643-3076), **La Hacienda** (Tel. 643-3191), or the **Hollywood Nightclub** (Tel. 643-1703). Ladies of the night may accost you in the vicinity of the **Beatle Bar**. Use one hand to guard your wallet and the other to guard the family jewels!

Avoid anyplace with the word "nightclub" in the name because in Costa Rica this almost always means a hostess bar where girls hustle you to buy over-priced drinks in exchange for their "company."

Manuel Antonio/Quepos

There are lots of nightspots in Manuel Antonio and nearby Quepos. They generally start late, and the trendiest don't get going until after midnight. **Arco Iris** (Tel. 777-0449) features DJs. **Monchados** has reasonably-priced Mexican and seafood and occasional live music.

Billy Beach's (Tel. 777-1557) is the bar at **Karola's** and hands out potent margaritas. **La Bodeguita, La Cantina, Epi Centro** and others rock until late. For gambling, there are casinos at the **Hotel Kamuk** in Quepos (Tel. 777-0379), and in the **Hotel Bybloss** in Manuel Antonio.

Puerto Jiménez

There is almost no place to party in Puerto Jiménez. Some would send you to **Juanita's Beer Garden** but I won't do that: they have no beer, no garden and no apologies. Instead, you need to drive outside town about six miles or so towards Matapalo and hang out at Martina's **Buena Esperanza,** the hippest spot for a hundred miles in any direction. It's just a sleepy little open-air bar on the side of the road but it rocks on the weekends.

The **Pearl of the Osa**, next to Iguana Lodge, has pasta and live music on Friday nights.

SPORTS & RECREATION

FISHING

Costa Rica is a world-class fishing destination. Although some fish the fresh water of Lake Arenal, most of the excitement is concentrated in the northern Caribbean for tarpon and snook, and on the Pacific side for sailfish, marlin and roosterfish. You pretty much have to stay in one of the all-inclusive fishing lodges to bag a tarpon. **Parismina** and **Barra del Colorado** are the spots.

Fishing lodges in the southern Pacific area are some of the best in the country. There are no fishing lodges as such in the central and northern Pacific region but there are dozens of charter boats and several hotels primarily dedicated to anglers.

You could let **Costa Rica Outdoors** (www.costaricaoutdoors.com; Tel. 800/308-3394 US,) handle the whole thing: they specialize in fishing packages.

Caribbean Coast

The lodges on the Caribbean side are clustered around Parismina and Barra del Colorado. You can only get to them by boat or small plane. None of them are in the category of "luxury" but they are all comfortable, with AC and wonderful food. Your chances of catching fish are about the same at any of them. All are steeped in "character."

Rio Parismina Lodge is one of the oldest and most famous of the fishing lodges in Costa Rica. Texan Judy Heidt runs Rio Parismina efficiently and with style. The rooms are comfortable and the boats and tackle top-notch. The buffet-style meals are good and the booze flows freely. The lodge is just minutes away from the snook and tarpon (locally called *sábalo*) action. *Info:* www.riop.com. Tel. 800/338-5688 US.

Jungle Tarpon Lodge. A small (four rooms), newer lodge near the river mouth, Jungle Tarpon specializes in eco-activities for non-fishing family members. Boats and tackle are good. Most of

How Much Will That Fishing Trip Cost?

Big-time sport fishing is **not cheap**. Charter boats on the Pacific coast run from a low of $650 a day on up to over $4,500 (for one day!). Most charters can take from four to six people with comfort. You can arrange to fish in local craft called *pangas* for much less. Larger boats are usually safer and more comfortable, with life vests, radios and extensive fish-oriented electronic goodies.

Dedicated fishing lodges on the southern Pacific and northern Caribbean coasts sell multi-day, all-inclusive packages that usually include two nights in a hotel in San José, transportation by air and boat to and from the lodge, food, lodging, all the booze you can glom, and as much time as possible fishing. Prices run from $2,500 to $3,500 for four full days fishing. An overnight trip for much less would be possible. Call or e-mail the lodges and ask about specials. If they have an empty boat, you may be able to work something out.

the guides fish live bait, although some lures are used on the river. The rooms are nice and air-conditioned. *Info:* www.jungletarpon.com. Tel. 800/544-2261 US.

Rio Colorado Lodge. Dan Wise, a likeable Mississippi lawyer, runs the loaded-with-charm, dripping-with-character Rio Colorado. He is everywhere at once, making sure guests are comfortable, boats are well stocked and tackle is in good repair. The rooms have been modernized and are air-conditioned. Don't miss his mama's recipe fried chicken. World record tarpon and snook are on the fishing bill of fare. *Info:* www.riocoloradolodge.com. Tel. 232-4063, 231-5987, 800/243-9777 US.

Silver King Lodge. Probably the nicest of all the lodges, Silver King has made a real effort to upgrade rooms and facilities. Their pool and Jacuzzi are super. They are now offering massages and spa treatments. Boats and tackle are the best. Food is spectacular even though they recently lost their star cook to a family imbroglio. *Info:* www.silverkinglodge.com. Tel. 381-1403, 800/847-3474 US.

Sad About the Samay

Sad to say, I can no longer recommend the Samay Lagoon Lodge. Sometimes known as the Kahlua or Samal Lodge, it is terminally run-down, and I have heard reports of guests being ripped off. There is an interesting story here, but not for a family audience. Avoid it.

Casa Mar. Hank Williams Jr. hangs out scratching Elvis the coonhound behind the ears as he sips umbrella drinks and talks about tarpon and snook. This is the oldest fishing lodge anywhere, and the celebrities and old-timers love it. A change of ownership since the death of the founder has changed little. It's still great. They just leave the bar open for the guests to do what they will. *Info:* www.casamarlodge.com. Tel. 433-9287, 433-8834, 800/543-0282 US.

Captain Eddy Brown is based in the Tortuguero area, and is well-known on the coast for the quantity of over-100-pound tarpon hauled in aboard his 19-foot center console, twin Yamaha **Bull Shark**. Book in advance, and he'll come and pick you up at your lodge. *Info:* Tel. 383-6097, 382-3350.

Jacó
Captain Tom's Sport Fishing operates out of the marina at Los Sueños, and Tom is one of the most successful captains on the coast. He works a 37' Defender and routinely helps clients release 10 to 20 sailfish daily. Marlin and dorado (the local name for the fish formerly known as dolphin or mahi-mahi) are also on his menu. The boat is roomy and fast enough to get out to where the big ones are. *Info:* Tel. 643-3995.

Quepos

Quepos is a world-class fishing destination, and anglers come from all over the world for sailfish, marlin, wahoo, tuna, dorado and Costa Rica's unique roosterfish. Numerous charter outfits will take you on half-day or full-day trips. Prices run from around $675 on up for a full-day trip, which includes tackle, bait and lunch. Most boats take up to four anglers, but some companies can accommodate larger groups. Most of these companies also arrange packages that include hotels, meals and local transportation. Some offer sightseeing boat rides as well. Try either **Quepos Sailfishing Charters**, Tel. 800/603-0015, or **Costa Rica Dreams**, www.costaricadreams.com; Tel. 637-8942.

Puerto Jiménez

Independent captain **Mike Hennessy** operates out of Puerto Jiménez, and is a real pro with his own new boat. Captain Mike is the recommended captain for many of the area lodges, so call well in advance for reservations. He can arrange for pickup. *Info:* Tel. 382-7796.

Crocodile Bay, located near the airport in Puerto Jiménez, is the most professionally run fishing lodge in the country. The tackle and boats are newish and top quality. Big boats, little boats, spinning or trolling tackle, they have it. Most fishing is done with live bait and teasers. This guarantees a good hook-up ratio. Captains and mates speak English.

You Wanna Eat It?

Most fishing operations in Costa Rica practice catch and release. You might keep a few filets of tuna or dorado for the table, but that prize billfish or rooster will survive to swim another day, thanks to local guides' skill at returning game fish to the water unharmed.

The rooms are large and modern, with everything you would expect to find in a nice US hotel somewhere. The all-inclusive packages are a good deal, with huge buffets, free-flowing bar, transportation in and out of San José and all the fishing you can handle. The best roosterfish action in the world starts about 500 feet from their dock. Sails, marlin, dorado and tuna choke the waters offshore. *Info:* www.crocodilebay.com. Tel. 735-5631, 800/733-1115 US.

Golfito
There are two serious fishing lodges close to Golfito:

Roy's Zancudo Lodge. Roy Ventura, the "father of Costa Rican sport-fishing," has a fleet of ten 25-foot center-console boats, and operates one of the nicest lodges in the country. *Info:* www.royszancudolodge.com. Tel. 776-0008, 877/529-6980 US. Playa Zancudo.

Golfito Sailfish Rancho is one of the country's best known fishing lodges, located a couple of bays north of Golfito. All-inclusive packages start at $1,810 per person for 3 days of fishing. *Info:* www.golfitosailfish.com. Tel. 800/824-1255 US.

DIVING
Although there is some coral to be found in the southern Caribbean area, most of the diving in Costa Rica is on sea life-rich rock mounds in the Pacific. Due to lots of plankton in the water, visibility is not unlimited, but the amount of exotic sea life visible is quite impressive. Encounters with whale sharks and manta rays are common. The **Papagayo** area and **Drake Bay** are where most of the action is.

Cocos Island is a world-famous place for swimming with hammerhead sharks and large pelagics. You have to take a liveaboard several hundred miles offshore for that pleasure.

Caribbean
There are a few dive operators in Cahuita, Puerto Viejo and Manzanillo. The better reefs are to the south.

Reef Runners offers two-tank dives for $60. Surprisingly, they don't require you to be certified to dive—they will give you a temporary certificate. *Info:* Tel. 750-0480.

Aquamor Talamanca Adventure does two-tank boat dives out of Manzanillo for a mere $55. *Info:* Tel. 759-9012.

Nicoya Area

Agua Rica Diving Center is in Tamarindo, taking divers to Islas Catalinas and other hot spots. Resort course and night dives are available. *Info:* Tel. 653-0094.

Ocotal Beach Marina operates just outside Coco in the Ocotal Resort. These are the guys to go with if you want to swim with the manta rays or get gobbled up by bull sharks. *Info:* www.ocotalresort.com. Tel. 670-0321.

Tom's Adventure Diving is in Playa Carillo. *Info:* Tel. 656-0061.

Manuel Antonio Area

Costa Rica Adventure Divers operates dive trips and PADI training. The Quepos area is not particularly noted for diving, but some great dives are to be had. If you are really hard-core you can arrange for trips a little further afield from Quepos. *Info:* Tel. 777-0234.

Drake Bay

Most of the diving is done around a hump a mile or so off Caño Island. The visibility is not great, but there are plenty of fish. Snorkeling or diving with dolphins is always popular. Two of the lodges specialize in diving.

La Paloma has the best diving platform in the area and all the equipment you'll need. It's also a wonderful jungle lodge. *Info:* www.lapalomalodge.com. Tel. 293-7502.

Jinetes de Osa is a comfortable lodge in Drake Bay catering to divers. *Info:* www.drakebayhotel.com. Tel. 800/317-0333 US.

Isla del Coco

The only way to get to Isla del Coco (aka Cocos Island) for diving is on one of the liveaboards that take people on week or ten-day dive trips. The dive is famous for hammerhead sharks and pelagics. Experienced divers only, please!

Go to **Undersea Hunter**, www.underseahunter.com; Tel. 228-6613, 800/203-2120 US, or **Okeanos Aggressor**, www.aggressor.com; Tel. 800/348-2628 US.

RAFTING

Most rafting is done on the **Pacuare** and **Reventazón** rivers, and put-in points for both are easily accessible from the San José area. Outfitters usually arrange for all transportation to and from your hotel, food, etc. You can go on one-day or overnight trips.

Some rafting is done from Manuel Antonio on the Savegre. The Corobici, Sarapiquí, Naranjo and El General rivers are also open for rafters.

Two companies dominate the rafting scene and are quite experienced. **Costa Rica Expeditions** (www.costaricaexpeditions.com; Tel. 257-0766) is the oldest and most respected rafting operator. **Rios Tropicales** (www.riostropicales.com; Tel. 233-6455, 866/722-8273 US) is a good competitor.

Soaking Wet?

Rafting is guaranteed to get you soaking wet. That's okay. Outfitters will carry your dry stuff in sealed, waterproof bags.

ZIP LINES

If you must do the zip line thing, try not to scream. **Zip lines** are available in almost all parts of the country. Realize that although some operators call their thing a "canopy tour," you don't get much time to actually examine the canopy, and most wildlife will be miles away from where tourists go screaming through the jungle. And we do scream.

To zip through the rain forest in Monteverde, try **Selvatura** (Tel. 645-5929), one of the more popular zip line operators. The **Original Canopy Tour** (Tel. 291-4465), in Monteverde and Tabacón, is probably the first of the zip companies.

BIRDING

Twitchers have a large choice of destinations where they will be certain to add significantly to their life lists. The most talked-about destination is **Monteverde** to see the resplendent quetzal, but it's overrated. There are far too many tourists, and the park is jammed. For that particular bird, a better choice would be the cloud forests around **Chirripó National Park** where you can choose from over 400 bird species including hummingbirds, eagle, red-tailed hawk, volcano hummingbird, black guan, crowned wren-thrush, acorn woodpecker, and not just any old trogon but an elegant trogon.

Other birding hot spots are **Tortuguero, Tiskita, Corcovado, Ecolodge San Luis & Biological Station**, and **Selva Bananito Lodge**. My favorite is **Trogon Lodge** near Chirripó National Park. **Carara**, though heavily touristed, is also worth a visit.

SURFING

Costa Rica is justifiably one of the top surfing destinations in the world. There are four or five primary hot spots you'll see surfers heading for with boards strapped to the tops of their SUVs.

La Salsa Brava is one wicked wave in the Caribbean south of Cahuita, in an area of dreadlocks, spliffs and curried goat.

Nicoya has dozens of fantastic surf spots with the most famous being **Witches Rock** in the Papagayo area. Watch out for crocs.

Jacó is close to San José, has good surf and a bar scene, so there is more surf stuff going on there than anywhere else. It is not really hip though. If you are gnarly, you don't go to Jacó.

Very hip and secret is the place known as **Punta Matapalo** on the tip of the Osa Peninsula. There are several places in Costa Rica called Matapalo but *this* is the one the surfers revere. The waves can get downright dangerous at times. There are no hotels or much of anyplace nice to stay except big-buck jungle lodges. There is only one bar or restaurant, which is **Martina's**, probably the hippest place in the whole country. People camp in the bushes or buddy up with someone renting a small house.

The very hippest surf spot of them all is **Pavones**, with its consistent quarter-mile-long left break. It's just a tiny village way out in the sticks near the Panamanian border. There is *nothing* going on here other than surfing, dude.

The web site at www.surf-costarica.com has lots of information about the surf scene, including current surf conditions and a list of "surf hotels."

MOUNTAIN BIKING

For serious, serious bikers, Cornelio Gonzalez's **Bike & Dreams** (Tel. 777-4389) guides biking tours in and around Manuel Antonio. For the physically able (not me) he takes groups up mountain trails from the coast to Chirripó. But you need to be fit for that one. The ride back down is tough, too.

GOLF

Costa Rica has several championship courses, all with wonderful tropical foliage, spectacular mountain or ocean vistas, and a bit of jungle wildlife to lend an air of adventure.

Operators of golf tours and websites with information on Costa Rican golf include:
- www.costaricagolftours.com
- www.golfcr.com
- www.worldgolf.com/travel/cosrica.html
- www.golfincostarica.com

Central Valley

The country's oldest 18-hole course is at the **Cariari Country Club** near San José, built in the 70s. Unless you have a Costa Rican friend, you won't get to play this beautiful par-71 course, as it's now a private country club.

Also in the Central Valley is **Valle del Sol**, a 6,750-yard par-72 course. Designed by Tracy May, it has a uniquely Costa Rican flavor, with fifteen small lakes (watch out for crocodiles), tropical trees and panoramic views of the Irazú, Barva and Poás volcanoes.

Nicoya Peninsula

In the 1990s, a parade of famous designers built several excellent oceanfront courses on the Nicoya Peninsula:

Garra de Leon, at the lavish Paradisus Playa Conchal resort, is a 7,030-yard course that was designed by Robert Trent Jones II. Watch the monkeys — they may steal your balls.

Just down the coast are **Hacienda Pinilla Golf & Country Club**, a 7,274-yard Mike Young design, the **Royal Pacific Golf & Country Club** (6,802 yards, Ron Garl), and **Los Sueños**. At the resort of the same name (see *Best Sleeps*), this 6,707-yard course was designed by Ted Robinson. This glamorous resort is also home to big-bucks fishing tournaments.

13. PRACTICAL MATTERS

AIRPORTS/ARRIVALS

Costa Rica's largest airport is **Juan Santamaría International Airport** (SJO), which is located near the San José suburb of Alajuela. Several major US airlines fly there from various hubs, including Houston, Miami and Atlanta. Costa Rica's national airline, Lacsa, is now a member of the TACA group (www.taca.com) and also offers service from the US. As of this writing, US airlines offer better connections and prices.

Expedia (www.expedia.com), Orbitz (www.orbitz.com) Travelocity (www.travelocity.com) and other similar Web resources are very useful for researching airfares. You can compare different routings and dates, and find the lowest fares available, usually the same as what a travel agent can find for you.

Personally, I don't use search engines to actually book travel, for two reasons. First, they will tack on an extra fee ($5 or so) for booking flights through their site, but you can just as easily book your flights online at the airline's website, once you've decided on an itinerary. Second, if you need to make any changes to your reservation, or if there is any dispute, you must deal with the search engine company, which often has more restrictive policies and higher fees for changes. Airlines and hotels will politely decline to assist you with any changes to a booking made through a search engine.

You may or may not be able to get a better deal on airfare by booking a package deal including lodging and tours through a travel agent or tour company (see below).

There are several ways to get from Juan Santamaría Airport to your destination. As you leave the terminal, just before you get outside to the sidewalk, there is a booth on the left that sells taxi vouchers for about $16. The designated taxis are right outside the door. Regular taxis are available to the right. The trip to central San José takes about a half hour, with good traffic, and costs around $20 in a regular taxi. Some of the upscale hotels have free shuttles. **Interbus** (www.interbusonline.com; Tel. 283-5573) and **Grayline** (www.graylinecostarica.com; Tel. 220-2126) operate shuttles between the airport and some of the major hotels for about $10 per person. There's also a public bus that costs about 50 cents (the stop is on the highway directly in front of the terminal). There are several car rental agencies at and near the airport.

Changing money at the change booths in the airport is a rip-off — you'll get 10% to 15% less than anywhere else. Pay for the taxi ride into town in US dollars at the booth, and change money at a bank in town (or, better yet, use an ATM to get some local currency).

Most flights arrive late in the day, so nearly all visitors spend a night in the area, and then get an early start the next day to fly or drive to their beach or rain forest destination. If this is your plan, you'll probably find it much more convenient to stay in one of several attractive lodgings in the area of Alajuela or Heredia, near the airport, avoiding central San José (see *Best Sleeps*).

San José has a second airport, **Tobías Bolaños Airport** (SYQ), which is more commonly referred to as **Pavas**, after the name of the part of San José where it is located. This is the main hub for the domestic airline **Nature Air**. Pavas Airport is about a 30-minute taxi ride from the main airport.

There is a second internal airline called **SANSA**, which flies from the main international airport, Juan Santamaría. Their terminal is a short walk from the main international terminal. You'll have to carry your bags. Both airlines only allow 30 pounds of luggage on internal flights.

There's a fairly new international airport near **Liberia** (LIR), in the northwest of the country, which is also served by several US airlines. Flying here instead of San José would be a good choice if you plan to visit the nearby Nicoya Peninsula or Rincón de la Vieja National Park. There are taxis available at the airport, as well as a

Cuban Cigars, Anyone?

It should come as no surprise that the most popular cigars in Costa Rica are Cuban. Many restaurants and hotels have them in stock. Costa Ricans, and visitors, are free to enjoy wonderful Cuban cigars and rum. As a US citizen you can buy and smoke them guilt-free — just don't try to take them back to the US with you. Customs agents recognize them by the paper rings.

public bus to downtown Liberia. Most lodges are happy to arrang for a van from the airport, which may be the most convenient option. There's some information about flight schedules and facilities at www.liberiacostaricainfo.com.

CRUISES

Quite a few cruise ships are visiting Costa Rica these days, but most of them follow the usual cruise ship routine, stopping at only one port in the country and running quick day tours of activities close to the port. East coast cruises tend to stop at Limón, while the West coast cruises stop at Puntarenas — neither are very interesting towns, but they're convenient for wonderful day trips.

A few smaller cruise lines offer more interesting Costa Rica-oriented trips. **Cruisewest** offers a particularly nice cruise on a small 120-passenger ship that stops on both coasts of Costa Rica, and passes through the Panama Canal. Some of their cruises include stops in other parts of Panama as well. On board are scientists from Harvard and other prestigious institutions who lead hikes and give talks on tropical biology, birds and wildlife, conservation and other topics of interest to more discerning travelers. **Cruisewest** also offers a weeklong trip just to Costa Rica.

Lindblad Expeditions also runs a small ship with naturalists on staff, which does an eight-day cruise of Costa Rica's Pacific coast, as well as longer itineraries that include Panama. Cruise lines that offer stops in Costa Rica include:

- **Cruisewest,** www.cruisewest.com; Tel. 800/580-0072.
- **Cunard,** www.cunard.com; Tel. 800/7cunard.
- **Holland America,** www.hollandamerica.com; Tel. 800/426-0327.
- **Lindblad Expeditions,** www.expeditions.com; Tel. 212/765-7740, 800/397-3348.
- **MSC Cruises,** www.msccruisesusa.com; Tel. 954/772-6262.
- **Orient Lines,** www.orientlines.com; Tel. 800/333-7300.
- **Princess Cruises,** www.princess.com; Tel. 800/774-6237.
- **Regent Seven Seas Cruises,** www.theregentexperience.com; Tel. 877/505-5370.
- **Seabourn Cruise Line,** www.seabourn.com; Tel. 800/351-9595.
- **Windstar Cruises,** www.windstarcruises.com; Tel. 800/258-7245.

PACKAGE TOURS

Lots of companies offer package tours, whether it's an all-inclusive deal including airfare from the States, or for part of your trip within Costa Rica. Even if you're the independent type, you may want to consider a package tour, at least for part of your trip. By coordinating charter flights and ground transportation, a tour company can get you to remote areas fairly quickly, eliminating much of the hassle. Here are some of the best of the large tour companies.

Costa Rica Expeditions (www.costaricaexpeditions.com) is perhaps the largest and best-known operator in the country. They manage several lodges, located in some of the best wildlife areas in the country: Monteverde, Tortuguero and Corcovado (see *Best Sleeps*). They can arrange anything there is to do in Costa

Rica, from a morning trip to a coffee plantation to a weeklong trek through the wilderness. Costa Rica Expeditions is best known as the original organizer of rafting trips in Costa Rica. Some of their most popular tours are their **"multi-sport" tours** involving rafting, surfing, hiking and a variety of other sporty activities. One of the things they do best is put together small groups of like-minded travelers of similar ages for hikes through Corcovado National Park, making all arrangements for food and lodging at the ranger station and at their wonderful Corcovado Lodge Tent Camp.

Insight Costa Rica (www.insightcostarica.com; Tel. 383-2597) is a small Alajuela-based company that arranges rural, community-based visitor experiences. Indigenous lifestyles are explored and presented to their tours. The "road less traveled" takes their visitors to out-of-the-way sites and activities based on a rural, sustainable lifestyle.

One of the larger agencies in Costa Rica, San José-based **Swiss Travel Service** (www.swisstravelcr.com; Tel. 282-4898) specializes in incentive and group travel.

Costa Rica Outdoors (www.costaricaoutdoors.com; Tel. 282-6743, 800/308-3394 US) focuses on full fishing packages, arranging flights, ground transportation, lodging and charter services. If you are a hard-core angler, they can arrange for you to spend several days dragging in tarpon on the Caribbean coast followed by several days tugging on sailfish in the Pacific. They are also a good choice for general tourism throughout the country.

Probably the number two tour company in Costa Rica, **Horizontes** (www.horizontes.com; Tel. 222-2022) offers group and individual travel plans. Their approach is to send their tours to the hotels and local tour operators they have experience with throughout the country.

International Adventures Unlimited (www.intladventures.com; Tel. 800/990-9738 US) specializes in upscale adventure travel, including whitewater rafting, kayaking, horseback riding and hiking throughout the country.

Guided tours of all kinds are big, big business in Costa Rica. Wildlife observation tours are the big banana, but all kinds of sports and activities are on offer as well. Horseback riding, mountain biking, kayaking, canoeing, whitewater rafting, caving, climbing and rappelling, underwater basket weaving...you name it, you can do it on a guided tour.

I highly recommend visiting the forest in the company of a **local guide**. You'll see much more, and learn much more about the area, than you would on your own. The best forest experiences are usually going to happen in small groups. The fewer people on your jungle hike the better — you'll be quieter and therefore see more wildlife, and the guide can spend more time answering your questions and addressing your particular areas of interest. There are four ways to go about arranging tours:

1) You can **book a package** that includes flights, hotels, meals and guides, over the web or with a local or Costa Rican travel agency before you even leave home. If you want to visit one of the more remote regions, and have limited time, this is your best option, though it probably won't be the cheapest.

2) Each of the major national parks has a pool of **licensed guides**, who take a three-year college course to become naturalist tour guides. You can sometimes just show up at the ranger station and arrange for a guide, but at the more popular parks, you'll be wiser to call ahead and make a reservation.

3) Every hotel in the country is familiar with the **local tours** that are on offer, and will be happy to help you make arrangements. They may tack on an extra fee.

4) In the more touristed areas, **freelance tour operators** hang around the beach or the main street and offer their services.

Inevitably, the flood of tourists looking for something to do has encouraged thousands of locals to get into the tour business. Some tours are excellent, and some are quite lame. We hear plenty of stories from travelers who got talked into overpriced tours that were far less exciting than advertised. There are lots of dubious "activities," which may sound tempting to families with smaller kids (whose patience for wildlife treks is likely to be limited). How to avoid wasting your time? Compare notes with other travelers, ask for lots of details, and be skeptical of recommendations from hotel clerks, especially if the tour operator happens to be a cousin.

Personally, I feel that precious time in Costa Rica is best spent seeing the unique attractions that the country has to offer (and there are *plenty*), not engaging in activities that you could just as easily do back in the United States. But that's just my opinion, so if you want to rappel inside of a hollow tree, visit a cave or go on a Tarzan tour, don't let me stop you.

GETTING AROUND
By Air
Roads in most of Costa Rica are crummy, and in some areas they are non-existent, so travel by small plane is a popular option. If you want to see a lot in a short time, it's the best way to travel. Two domestic airlines, **SANSA** (www.flysansa.com; Tel. 221-9414) and **Nature Air** (www.natureair.com; Tel. 299-6000) offer flights to a couple dozen destinations around the country. Reasonably priced charter companies can fly you to even the most remote jungle lodges. If you have more than four people in your group it may be a better deal to arrange for a charter. Charters are usually more convenient, leaving and arriving at a time to suit you. Some small airports are served only by charter.

Both domestic airlines serve most of the same destinations within Costa Rica. Nature Air also flies to Granada in Nicaragua and Boca del Toro in Panama. SANSA is part of a larger business group (Grupo Taca) and can arrange for connections to Panama, Nicaragua, Honduras, Cuba and Guatemala. Remember that Nature Air flies only from Pavas and SANSA flies only from the main international airport. Currently, only Nature Air flies to Carate in the Osa Peninsula. There are other, small airstrips served only by private charters.

Other than the three main airports described above, the rest are little more than landing strips with few or no facilities. Some of the smallest are nothing but a reasonably level field of grass. Little boys with sticks drive the cows off just before each landing.

Both airlines only allow **30 lbs. of luggage total** — checked and carry-on.

Car Rental

Renting your own car offers the maximum in flexibility, but the poor state of the roads puts some people off. Anything that doesn't have 4-wheel drive is likely to be inadequate once you get off the major highways (and if you don't plan to drive off the major highways, there's little reason to rent a car). Fortunately, most rental agencies have a good selection of 4WD vehicles, from cute little Subarus to hulking SUVs.

I've had good experiences with **Europcar** (www.europcar.com; Tel. 257-1158) and **Toyota** (Tel. 258-5797). You can rent an older, cheaper car from **4x4 Rent a Car** (www.4x4rentacar.com; Tel. 441-0000). You'll save a lot of hassle, and possibly some money as well, if you reserve a rental car online before leaving home.

Rental cars are not cheap in Costa Rica. The government has a monopoly on insurance, and all car rentals include the cost of mandatory insurance. Even if you already have your own insurance through your regular insurance company or through your credit card, you'll have to pay for the government insurance.

Gasoline usually costs about the same as it does in the US. Filling stations (*bombas* or *gasolineras*) are rare outside of towns, so it's prudent to top up whenever you see one. The government runs all the gas stations, so the prices are generally the same all over the country. There is no need to shop around for the best price.

Police with radar are common and are quite willing to hand out speeding tickets. Be very careful approaching villages if you are cruising fast on the highway. Speed limits are almost always much lower in towns and the cops (*las pacas*), often spend all day hanging around by the side of the highway with their radar guns.

Taxis

Taxis are reasonably priced and convenient. Within towns, they're the best way to get around. After dark in San José and other cities, they're the only safe way to get around. In San José, drivers are theoretically required to charge by the meter (called a *maría*), but elsewhere fares are usually negotiable. A word to the wise: any time you take a taxi in the developing world, be sure to agree on a fare *before* riding anywhere.

A taxi can also be an affordable way to get to rural destinations, or just to take a tour around the countryside, especially if you're with a group.

Probably the best way to enjoy your trip around Costa Rica is to hire a driver and their vehicle. If you have more than four or so people in your party it becomes an economically viable alternative.

For example, **Esterling Alfaro** (www.InsightCostaRica.com; Tel. 430-2630) has his own 12-passenger air-conditioned van, and is available for one- or multi-day trips around the country. He knows all the little out-of-the-way places to stop for a good bite to eat and explains, tells stories and educates as much or as little as you like. For visitors planning trips with specific interests such as birding, visiting national parks, or rural tourism, he will be happy to put together suggestions and quote a price.

Buses

Both **Interbus** (www.interbusonline.com; Tel. 283-5573) and **Grayline** (www.graylinecostarica.com; Tel. 220-2126) have frequent scheduled service between most Costa Rican tourist destinations, using small to medium-sized tourist buses. Prices are usually excellent, and they will often pick you up at your hotel.

The public bus system covers most of the country, is reasonably punctual, and is very cheap. Some popular tourist areas are served by faster (and pricier) air-conditioned express buses in addition to the usual Central American torture buses (some of which are old school buses).

BANKING & CHANGING MONEY

Costa Rica's monetary unit is the *Colón* (plural *Colones*). At press time, the interbank exchange rate was 537 to the Dollar (**one US Dollar = 537 Colones**). See www.oanda.com for current rates.

Most travelers don't really understand how currency exchange works, and this ignorance can cost you money. Here's the straight scoop. *Every time* you change currencies, you pay a fee in the form of the *spread* between the buy and sell exchange rates. The *interbank rate*, the rate at which banks exchange money among themselves, lies midway between the buy and sell rates, so the bank earns a fee on *every transaction*. Some currency-exchange places also charge a small fixed commission, the purpose of which is to prevent you from comparing rates between different exchange outlets. Even if a place trumpets "No Commission!" you're still paying a fee. To see if you're getting a good deal or a bad deal, look at the spread.

Credit cards and ATM cards offer the best spreads (about 2% from the interbank rate for credit cards, 3-4% for ATMs), and using them in Costa Rica has gotten much easier in recent years. **ATMs** are fairly common, and nowadays most medium-sized towns have an ATM that will accept US cards belonging to one of the major ATM networks (Honor, Cirrus, etc). In the past, most Costa Rican ATMs accepted local bank cards only.

Most substantial tourist-oriented businesses will accept **credit cards** (Visa is far more widely accepted than MasterCard or American Express). Smaller places may not accept cards, and some places will tack on an extra fee for using plastic (technically, this is against the credit card companies' rules, but places do it anyway).

Changing money at banks is a bureaucratic nightmare, but they may offer the best exchange rates for cash. Most hotels will gladly change money for you, but will probably offer a somewhat unfavorable rate. Changing money at the change booths in the airport is a *big* rip-off (see above). As for the touts offering to change money on the street, don't even talk to them.

Most banks will accept only US Dollars (UK Pounds or Euros *maybe*, but anything else, forget it). Travelers' checks are not widely accepted, and are subject to extra fees.

Most businesses will accept US Dollars (and give your change in *Colones*), but you may get a worse price than you would if you paid in local currency. While large hotels and tour operators follow the daily exchange rates, smaller businesses tend to use a rough-and-ready-rate, such as 500 *Colones* to the Dollar. Depending on the current interbank rate, this may be a decent deal or a bad deal.

Costa Rican *Colones* are not convertible outside the country, so remember to change any leftover cash back to Dollars before leaving, or squander it in the duty-free shop at the airport. The exchange desk at the airport will exchange no more than $50 worth at a time.

BUSINESS HOURS
Most businesses are open from around 9am to 5 or 6pm Monday through Friday, and perhaps Saturday morning. Hours tend to be longer in larger cities and tourist areas. Many businesses and offices close for two hours at lunchtime. Banks in small towns may have very limited hours. Most non-tourist-oriented businesses are closed on Sunday.

CLIMATE & WEATHER
Costa Rica has an amazing variety of climates for such a small country. Generally speaking, the Pacific north is hot and dry during the winter months, a little like California, but is rainy and humid the rest of the year. The south and the Caribbean coastal region have more typical tropical weather: hot, humid and rainy.

The Central Valley has consistently pleasant temperatures, always between 49 and 92 degrees Fahrenheit. High in the mountains, such as around Chirripó, it can actually get quite cold, even below freezing on occasion.

There are two main seasons. The **dry season** lasts from November through April, and is the main tourist season. The **"Green Season"** (which sounds more appealing than "rainy season") lasts from May through October, and sees far fewer tourists. Most areas of the country do get a lot of rain during this season, and some remote regions, especially in the south, can become almost inaccessible by road. However, other areas, such as the Pacific Northwest region, see far less rain. Prices can be much lower during the Green Season, and the crowds are gone.

CONSULATES & EMBASSIES

The **US embassy** is located in Pavas (Tel. 220-3939; www.usembassy.or.cr).

The **Canadian embassy** is in central San José (Tel. 296-4149; www.dfait-maeci.gc.ca/latin-america/sanjose).

The **UK embassy** is also in central San José (Tel. 225-4049; www.embajadabritanica.com).

ELECTRICITY

Costa Rica uses **110-volt AC**, the same as in the US, and the plugs are the same. Grounded (3-prong) plugs are not common, and the general level of electrical safety is low. Cheaper lodgings may feature "suicide showers," little electric heaters attached to the showerhead, sometimes with poorly insulated connectors (we've heard no reports of anyone actually being killed by one of these contraptions, which are also known as "widow makers," but *do not touch them*). Remote lodges get their power from generators, which may be turned off at night, and may deliver dodgy voltage.

EMERGENCIES & SAFETY

Crime

Compared to other Central American countries, Costa Rica is pretty safe, but thievery of various kinds does happen, and violent crime against tourists is not unheard-of. Follow a few precautions, and you should have no problems:

• As everyone will tell you, it isn't safe to walk around the streets of San José or other cities at night. Using the public bus system after dark may be dodgy as well. **At night, always take a taxi.**

• Never, ever leave any valuables in parked cars. In fact, in San José it's probably unwise to park anywhere other than a watched hotel parking lot.

• Be on the alert for **pickpockets** in any crowded situation, especially at airports, bus stations and such places. Not only cities, but also highly touristed parks such as Monteverde and Carara have their share of thieves.

• In some parks, **walking alone on isolated trails is not recommended**. Always check in at the ranger station, and hike in groups, preferably with a local guide.

• Walking on beaches at night is generally not a good idea.

I highly recommend a **money belt**. *Not* the external "fanny-pack," but a small flat belt that goes around your waist (there are similar things that go around your neck) *under your clothes*. With your passport, plane ticket and main cash stash zipped up out of sight, you can relax and enjoy your trip (of course, you keep a small roll of walking-around money in a pocket, so you never have to pull out your money belt in public). Money belts are available at any good luggage shop or (much cheaper) at discount stores.

As for those fanny-packs, they're famous around the world as magnets for thieves and con artists. Even if you don't plan to keep any valuables in it, I strongly urge you to leave it at home. A fanny pack shouts "opportunity!" to people whom you'd rather not meet. The sight of a fanny pack to a street hustler is like the sound of a can opener to a hungry cat.

Be on your guard whenever you hand over cash for tours and other local services. Make sure you're dealing with a legitimate employee, and get a receipt. When paying by credit card, keep a close eye on your card, and make sure any unused charge slips (for example, for a rental car deposit) are destroyed.

Petty theft is not the only type of crime to watch out for. **Con men** run various investment scams on tourists and retirees. If you're doing any kind of business, buying real estate or investing in the country, be extra careful to deal only with reputable firms, and, most definitely, seek advice from a local third party such as a lawyer or accountant before signing anything or parting with any dough.

Recently, several high-profile scams have been exposed, involving extremely high returns on cash investments. 30% return per month for investments of at least $100,000 is a typical offering. Of course, the monthly payments stop well before you've earned your original investment back. Be careful about pitches for depositing money in back street "banks." If it sounds too good to be true, it is.

In many Latin American countries the police are famous for demanding informal "fines," to be paid in cash on the spot, for real or imagined traffic violations. This behavior is rare in Costa Rica, but we have heard reports that it does occur. If you do get cited, don't give the cops any cash, but make sure they give you a paper traffic ticket, which you will have to pay at a bank.

Unlike some tropical vacation destinations, Costa Rica is not particularly tolerant of **marijuana** or **drugs**. Laws are just as strict as those in the US, or even more so. You may be offered *mota* or *ganja*, especially on the Rasta-flavored Caribbean coast, but buying on the street exposes you to many dangers, including being ripped off or turned over to the authorities.

If you travel with prescription drugs, be sure they are clearly labeled and, if possible, in the original containers (it's currently illegal to import prescription drugs into the US, and we've heard reports that customs agents have been zealously enforcing the rules).

Police can ask for ID at any time, so keep yours with you. On the roads, you may occasionally pass through a police checkpoint. Have your passport and the car's papers available.

Prostitution is legal in Costa Rica (as in most places outside the US), and "sex tourism" is big business. The meat market at the

Blue Marlin Bar at the Hotel del Rey in San José is world-famous. Abuse of minors is a sore point with the authorities, who do not want Costa Rica to gain a reputation as "another Thailand." Having sex with anyone under 18 is strictly illegal.

HEALTH

Costa Rica's health care system is decent. In fact, "health tourists" come here to get medical treatment at bargain rates, especially plastic surgery. There's a network of public hospitals throughout the country. **In an emergency, dial 911**, or 128 for an ambulance. For non-emergency health needs, you'll probably get better and quicker service from a private doctor or clinic, which you can find in the phone book (the Spanish for "doctor" is *médico*).

The health hazards here are the same ones you'll encounter when pursuing touristy activities in any tropical country. Be very careful about exposure to the sun: it can hurt you even on cloudy days. Pack *plenty* of insect repellent, with DEET (forget about milder remedies such as Skin-So-Soft—the mosquitoes down here will just laugh at that stuff).

Food and water are generally safe: Montezuma is less vengeful here than in some other tropical destinations. To be on the safe side, drink bottled water and use it to rinse any fruits that you don't peel or cook. No shots are required for travel to Costa Rica. Malaria and other tropical diseases are rare.

Poisonous snakes are common throughout the country, but **snakebites are rare**. When hiking in the forest, watch your step at all times, and don't stick your hand in anywhere it doesn't belong. A stout pair of **hiking boots** is a very good idea for several reasons. Slipping in the mud and spraining your ankle is more likely than getting bit by a *terciópelo*, and it could ruin your holiday.

Travelers with special health concerns should note that remote jungle lodges have limited ability to evacuate you in a medical emergency: if something happens to you, it could be hours or days before you get to a hospital.

ETIQUETTE

Ticos are great ones for **politeness** — when they meet, there's a great deal of handshaking, "how's the family?" and so forth, before any business gets discussed. Greet your new friends in the morning with *¿Cómo amaneció?* which literally means "How did you wake up?" The word *buenas* serves as an all-purpose greeting, short for the more formal *buenas mañanas/tardes/noches* (good night/afternoon/evening). See the "Essential Spanish" section at the end of this chapter for more pleasantries.

Ticos tend to be *a little* more punctual than some other Latin Americans, but don't get too upset when people show up fashionably late. The phrase *hora americana* means that something is supposed to happen more or less on time, whereas *hora tica* means the usual dithering around.

Tico? Gringo?

It is quite all right to call Costa Ricans *"Ticos"* (or *"Ticas"* if they are female). The term comes from the Costa Rican habit of adding the *-ico* or *-ica* diminutive ending to words. Formal Castilian speakers think the Ticos are a little too cutesy with their slang. You should also realize that it is not the least impolite for the Ticos to refer to us as **"Gringos"** (or *"Gringas"*). Most Latin Americans consider themselves to be *"Americans"* but realize that the word is usually reserved for people from the US. In Spanish, the word *"Estadounidense"* means someone from the United States. *"Norteamericano"* has a similar meaning, encompassing Canadians as well.

Even though you're in the tropics, please don't dress as if the whole country is a beach. At all-inclusive resorts and funky little tourist towns, beach bum attire is fine, but in places like banks, stores, etc. you'll notice that the locals wear long pants, shirts, and even jackets and ties, just as we do at home (some older guys wear the traditional *guayabera* shirt in lieu of a tie). Walking around in shorts and flip-flops marks you instantly as a tourist. Ticos almost always dress better then their North American visitors. If you see someone in ragged shorts or bathing suit and a t-shirt — it's a tourist. Flip-flops are

OK in most places but you may want to actually wear shoes in nice restaurants.

You might notice that Ticos rarely point at things with their fingers as we do in the US. Watch carefully and you'll see them pursing their lips and "pointing" with their lips and a head movement. Try it yourself: just make a kissy face (but don't actually make the kissy noise) and kind of bob your chin in the direction you wish to indicate. The locals won't think it's odd at all, but you might want to shed the habit before you go back to the office after your vacation.

HISTORY OF COSTA RICA – THE SHORT VERSION
You'll hear a good bit of speculation about why Costa Rica has **a long history as a peaceful democracy**, while so many other Latin American countries have histories full of interesting stuff like (I'm sorry, but it's true) Fascist and/or Communist dictators, narco-terrorism, military juntas and death squads. Whatever political conclusions you may draw, it's definitely true that Costa Rica's history is unique among the former Spanish colonies. This fairly benign history is part of the reason for Costa Rica's current prosperity and the typically peaceful personality of the Ticos themselves.

Columbus "discovered" Costa Rica September 11, 1502 on his fourth voyage, landing in the vicinity of Limón. As was customary at the time, the Spaniards immediately slaughtered everyone they encountered. Indigenous peoples such as the Chorotegas, Bruncas and Térrabas were killed, enslaved, infected, ejected and driven far into the mountains where their descendants and remnants of their culture can be found today.

A bold fellow named **Gil Gonzales Davila** came along a few years after Columbus and, noticing a few gold ornaments worn by some of the unfortunate remaining locals, named the place "Costa Rica" (Rich Coast). Although gold is still sought in a few areas of the country today, little gold was found during the days of the conquistadors.

Since there was little gold and little resistance to settlers, there was no need for actual "conquest," and the area became a quiet backwater, **ignored by European empire builders**. The few Spanish settlers established small subsistence farms, and developed a strong tradition of local autonomy and egalitarianism. The economy grew around growing sugar cane, coffee and bananas.

In contrast to other American colonies, there were few large-scale plantations, and thus no need to import Africans or other non-Spaniards as slaves. As a result, the population of Costa Rica today is relatively racially homogonous, with only small Black, indigenous and Asian communities.

In 1821, the **United Provinces of Central America** declared their independence from Spain. The loose federation never worked out, and in 1838 Costa Rica withdrew and became a sovereign country. Smart locals backed businessman **Braulio Carillo**, who turned out to be a benevolent founder and dictator. As such he is known as the Father of Costa Rica, somewhat like George Washington in the US.

Life went on more or less peacefully until the 1850s, when a scoundrel named **William Walker** came into the picture. In those days, if you had a small band of bloodthirsty and ruthless pals, and some guns and powder, you could march into a small country, declare yourself in charge, and begin to live the good life on the backs of whomever you could find in the area to oppress. *Filibuster* was the word used to describe this activity. Apparently, this is exactly what this Walker character had in mind, and he managed to pull it off in Nicaragua.

When he attempted to expand his empire to Costa Rica, the locals decided they were having none of it, spontaneously put together a "people's army" and routed his forces near the border, at a site now commemorated by Santa Rosa National Park (see Chapter 8). A teenager martyred himself in this operation, resulting in Costa Rica's independence day being known as Juan Santamaría Day in his honor.

Walker continued his evil ways up the coast for several more years until he was ignominiously shot in the head by the local police in a dusty, flyblown, two-mule village in Honduras. An alternative ending has him shot by a British naval officer who found him to be "a bit much." A proper Hollywood ending in either case. Several movies have been made about him, including *Walker*.

In 1889, a political faction attempted to foist a president on the populace and promptly faced a serious revolt. A direct election for President followed, beginning Costa Rica's tradition of peaceful elections, which has continued mostly uninterrupted to this day.

In 1948, a disputed presidential election led to a **civil war** that lasted 44 days and killed 2,000 people. However, the winning faction, in an event almost unique in human history, decided to implement reforms to serve the people. The leader of the rebels, **José Figueres Ferrer**, became president, and is today a national hero.

This wise leader immediately established a new constitution that guaranteed free elections and universal suffrage, declared international neutrality, disbanded the military, and nationalized insurance companies, postal services and banks. He then supervised a new, fair election, quit his office and retired. What a guy! He was so appreciated by the people they elected him president twice a few years later.

Democratic government has continued uninterrupted to the present day, with the administration of current president **Óscar Arias**. In 1987, Arias was awarded the **Nobel Peace Prize** for his help in ending the seemingly eternal civil wars in neighboring Nicaragua, Guatemala and El Salvador.

Elections in Costa Rica are noted as being particularly fair, peaceful and properly managed. School children are used to keep voters in lines. The close 2006 election between Óscar Arias and Ottón Solís was settled with little fuss by a manual recount, with Arias proclaimed the winner. Although Ticos complain about nepotism, general corruption and economic inequalities, there is little acrimony concerning their electoral process.

Thank goodness for a boring history!

LAND & PEOPLE
Costa Rica is located in Central America, on a narrow isthmus between the Caribbean Sea and the Pacific Ocean (only 75 miles from sea to sea at the narrowest point). Her neighbors are Nicaragua to the north and Panama to the south.

Mysterious Spheres

A few hundred mysterious stone spheres have been found in several parts of Costa Rica. Found when plowing fields mostly around Palmar and the Diquis River delta, the spheres vary from a few inches to more than eight feet in diameter. They are **perfectly round and smooth**, and have been dated between 800 and 1200 BC. The spheres can be seen used as yard art in suburban lawns and in museums around the country. You can see several large ones in a small park near the airport, opposite the end of the runway as you head towards San José. Who made them? Many of the largest ones seem to have been transported more than 20 miles from where they were quarried.

The backbone of the country is formed by several rugged mountain ranges, part of the range that runs all along the Pacific coast of America, from the Rockies to the Andes. In the north are the Guanacaste, Tilarán, and Central ranges, some of them active volcanoes, while to the south the Talamanca range includes the country's highest peak, **Cerro Chirripó** (12,530 feet).

Costa Rica has a huge variety of landscapes for such a small country (just 20,000 square miles or 51,100 square kilometers, about the same size as West Virginia), which has led several writers to describe it as a tiny continent in and of itself. Sand beaches and mangrove swamps, open savannah and impenetrable rain forest, coastal jungle, high cloud forest and even *paramo*, or "wet desert" – each forms its own unique ecosystem of animals and plants adapted to local conditions.

The **Central Valley** (Valle Central) is located on a high plateau with fertile soil and a pleasant temperate climate. It was here that the first major Spanish settlements were founded, and it's here that almost two thirds of the population lives today. Here is the capital, San José, and the smaller cities of Cartago, Alajuela and Heredia, with almost all the country's industry and most of the coffee plantations. It's a pleasant area of well-ordered farms and woodlands.

The **Pacific coast** is very rough, dotted with bays and little islands. The hilly **Nicoya Peninsula** in the north was for many years a sparsely-populated region of small villages, but today it is home to dozens of new real estate developments, as well as some of Costa Rica's most upscale resorts, with more on the way.

The steep coast south of Nicoya is the closest coastal area to the Central Valley, so it's no surprise that Costa Rica's biggest resort towns are here: Jacó, Quepos and Manuel Antonio. South along the coast sprawl vast palm-oil plantations with little company towns where the workers live.

In the southwest corner of the country is the **Osa Peninsula**, a remote and sparsely inhabited region that was once the haunt of loggers and gold miners. Today much of the region is nature preserve, the largest remaining area of primary forest on the Pacific coast of America.

The **Caribbean coast** is far smoother than the Pacific, with an almost continuous swath of wild and deserted beaches from Nicaragua to Panama. The northern Coast is very low, with a labyrinth of canals, marshes, wetlands and rain forest stretching for miles inland from the coast. Halfway down the coast is the country's second-largest city, the grubby port town of Limón.

Agriculture is an important and highly visible part of the economy, especially coffee in the Central Valley and bananas on both coasts, as well as pineapples, sugar, rice and beans (of course), and beef. However, Costa Rica is by no means a banana republic. On the contrary, the economic breakdown reads more like that of a typical "first-world" country: 9% agriculture, 30% industry and 61% services.

Small industries include microprocessors, food processing and textiles. Tourism is an ever-growing part of the economy, recently joined by modern services such as offshore banking and internet gambling.

Most of Costa Rica's four million people are poor by North American standards, but the country is one of Latin America's greatest success stories, with a per capita Gross Domestic Product (GDP) of $11,000 and a poverty rate of only 18%. The government provides a respectable roster of social services, including state-funded medical insurance and a social security plan. Levels of literacy and education are high.

The Ticos have **strong traditions of independence and egalitarianism**, which arise from the colonial past. The typical Latin American colony was a rigidly stratified society, with slaves at the bottom and wealthy plantation owners at the top. Not so in Costa Rica, where most people were of fairly pure Spanish blood, and all were poor but proud subsistence farmers who had to work together for the good of all. At least, that's the idealized version of history that informs the Tico self-image.

Unlike other countries in Central and South America, indigenous people make up only a small percentage of the population. 94% of Costa Ricans are *mestizos*, of mostly Spanish descent.

Only a few Blacks were brought to Costa Rica back in the slave days. Most of the Black folks (3% of the population) are descendents of Jamaicans who came in the 19th century to work on the banana plantations. In the bad old days, they were prohibited from spending the night in the Central Valley, which tended to concentrate their numbers on the southern Caribbean coast. Although the constitution of 1949 abolished legal discrimination, most of the blacks (or Creoles) continue to live in the region today.

Native Americans now make up only about one percent of Costa Rica's population. However, there are a few groups who still live somewhat as they did in pre-Colombian times in remote forest regions.

On the Nicoya peninsula, you can still find traces of the traditional culture of the **Chorotegas**, especially in the village of Guaitíl, famous for its traditional pottery. The **Borucas** live in remote settlements near the southern Pacific coast.

The most isolated indigenous tribes are the Cabécar and the Bribri Indians, who live a traditional lifestyle way up in the jungles north of the Talamanca mountain range.

Roman Catholics account for 76 percent of Costa Ricans. As elsewhere in Latin America, Catholicism is a major part of the culture. The Creoles of the Caribbean coast are traditionally Protestants, and a number of Evangelical denominations thrive throughout the country. Several groups belonging to traditional Christian sects have settled in the country, seeking a remote place far from the sinful USA. The best known are the Quakers who founded the town of Monteverde in the 1950s.

INTERNET ACCESS

Costa Rica is getting wired up rapidly. E-mail is a good alternative to the unreliable postal service. **RACSA** (www.racsa.co.cr) is the largest internet provider, offering both dial-up and broadband (cable) service. Internet cafés are common throughout the country. Many larger hotels offer internet service (with the exception of the more remote wilderness lodges, which may be out of reach of the telephone network). Some post offices also offer internet access for a fee. Wireless access in hotels is not uncommon.

There are a few internet cafés listed at www.cibercentro.com/costarica, and you can find more on some of the internet directory sites. See the list of Costa Rica-oriented internet directories and search engines at the end of this chapter.

LANGUAGE

The language of Costa Rica is **Spanish**, in its Latin American variant, which differs slightly from the Castilian Spanish spoken in Spain. It's not difficult to travel in Costa Rica without knowing a word of Spanish, as English is widely spoken in all tourist areas (in fact, you'll find that the owners of wilderness lodges and other tourist-oriented businesses are often from the US or Europe).

However, any experienced traveler will tell you that knowing a few key words will greatly enhance your trip. *Por favor* (please) and *gracias* (thank you) are the most useful, and using them liberally will smooth your way to a remarkable extent. And of course, you're sure to quickly learn the all-purpose Costa Rican expression *pura vida*.

If you do want to learn Spanish, Costa Rica is an excellent place to do so. Hundreds of **language schools** cater for beginners and experts, dabbling vacationers or long-term residents. Some offer accommodations in wonderful rain forest or beachside locations.

The **National Registration Center for Study Abroad** (www.nrcsa.com) is an organization that will help you choose and register for any of dozens of language schools around the world. They evaluate language schools, select the ones that they consider the best, and offer pre-registration to the schools on their approved list, which includes six schools in Costa Rica.

Other language schools include **Intensa** (www.intensa.com) near the university in San José; **CPI** (www.cpi-edu.com), with campuses in Heredia, Monteverde and Playa Flamingo; and **Escuela d'Amore** (www.escueladamore.com) near Manuel Antonio.

Some of the residents of the southern Caribbean coast speak a local dialect of English, similar to the Patois spoken in Jamaica. Several Native American languages such as Bribri and Cabécar are spoken at various places throughout the country.

NEWSPAPERS

Several newspapers in Spanish and at least one in English serve Costa Rica. Tourism-oriented newspapers come and go, but the

Tico Times is a solid and well-written English-language weekly. Visiting their web site (www.ticotimes.net) is an excellent way to get in the mood before your trip. Their weekly fishing report is a must-view for all anglers aiming at Costa Rica. *La Nación* is a conservative daily paper. *La Prensa Libre* and *La Republica* are other, perhaps less-conservative dailies.

PASSPORT REGULATIONS
Passports are required for entry. Citizens of the US, Canada and the UK (as well as most European countries) are permitted to stay in Costa Rica for up to 90 days without a visa. Citizens of Australia, New Zealand, South Africa and Ireland may stay for 30 days without a visa. For the complete list of visa requirements for different countries, see www.visitcostarica.com/ict/paginas/informacionturistica.asp.

If you want to stay for more than 90 days, the best thing to do is simply leave the country overnight and come back for another 90 days. It is possible to get an extension (*prórroga de turismo*) from the immigration office (*migración*), but the bureaucratic nightmares involved make this option impractical.

Officially, your passport must be valid for more than six months from the date of entry, or you will be refused admission.

There's a **departure tax** of $26 per person, which you must pay at the airport before checking in. The desk for paying the tax is at the far right end of the departure terminal. You have to show a receipt for the tax before you can check in, so be sure you get this done as soon as you arrive in the airport. Some hotels can collect the tax and give you a receipt ahead of time so you don't have to fool with this at the airport. You can pay in Dollars or Colones.

POSTAL SERVICES
Costa Rica's postal service (*correos*) is notoriously slow and inefficient. You can expect mail from Costa Rica to the States or Europe to take at least two weeks, if it arrives at all. When contacting hotels or tour operators in Costa Rica, use e-mail or fax if at all possible. For important packages, use FedEx or DHL, both of which have offices in San José.

San José's main post office is at Avenida 1, Calle 2. There's also a small postal museum. See www.correos.go.cr.

TELEPHONES

The telephone system is also a little on the crummy side, but serviceable. Cell phones are common, and you can even rent one for your visit.

The country code is 506. To call Costa Rica from the US, dial: 011 506 [local number].

Most phone booths use **phone cards**, which you can buy at grocery stores and newsstands. Phone cards are a bargain, and offer the cheapest way to call North America. Try to avoid making calls from hotels, which love to add a hefty markup to the price.

Another good way to call home is by calling the direct access number for your long-distance company, and using your calling card:

- AT&T: Tel. 0800 011 4114
- MCI: Tel. 0800 012 2222
- Sprint: Tel. 0800 013 0123

Many remote lodges are far from phone lines or cellular coverage, so the only option may be to use a satellite phone, which is quite expensive.

To call the US or Canada from CR, dial: 001 [area code and number].

An online telephone directory is at www.superpagescr.com.

You can send **faxes** at most post offices and hotels.

Blue "tourist phones" are starting to show up at hotels and some tourist attractions. These are clearly marked as being particularly for calls overseas and take only credit cards. Although convenient and easy to use, they are extremely expensive with even short calls to the US running over $30. Avoid them.

TIME

The time in Costa Rica is **equal to US Central Standard Time** (six hours behind Greenwich Mean Time, one hour behind Eastern Standard Time). However, they do not recognize Daylight Savings Time. The length of the days and nights doesn't vary much here in the tropics. It gets dark about 6pm every day, year round. Nicaragua tried Daylight Savings Time a couple of years ago but dropped it as almost everyone simply ignored it.

TIPPING

A **10% service charge is added to all restaurant bills,** so there's no need to do more than round up to the next even amount, unless service is exceptional. Taxi drivers don't usually expect tips. Porters should receive a little something. Many tour guides have come to expect tips, especially in tourist-swamped regions such as Monteverde, but you really needn't give them anything extra unless they go above and beyond the call of duty.

You may occasionally be approached by freelance porters, usually young kids (in a former age, they would have been called "blackguard boys") who hang around tourist areas and offer to carry your bags, guard your car while you're away, help you through the intricacies of buying a bus ticket, or other small services. Use your discretion as to whether they are to be trusted. If your tip is too small, they'll let you know.

TOURIST INFORMATION

The **Costa Rica Tourist Board** (Instituto Costarricense de Turismo, www.visitcostarica.com; Tel. 866-COSTARICA) has offices at the airport and at the Plaza de la Cultura in central San José. Their Web site has lots of information, including visa and entry requirements, customs, flights, hotels, tours, car rental and more, plus lots of maps and photos.

WATER

Tap water in larger cities is theoretically safe to drink, although I recommend sticking to bottled water to be on the safe side. Remote lodges may have dodgy water supplies, with low pressure and little or no hot water.

WEIGHTS & MEASURES

All measurements in Costa Rica use the metric system. Liquids are sold by the liter, which is a tiny bit more than a quart. Food is often sold by the gram. One kilogram is 2.2 pounds, and 100 grams of meat or cheese is about enough for a sandwich. Distance is measured in meters (about 39 inches) or kilometers (1.6 kilometers equals 1 mile).

Temperature is measured in Celsius degrees. 0° Celsius is freezing, or 32° Fahrenheit. 100° Celsius equals the boiling point of water, or 212° F.

Most people you'll meet in the tourist industry are familiar with our American system of measurement, so they will usually be able to give you a rough-and-ready conversion.

One hundred kilometers is roughly 60 miles. If the posted speed limit is 80 km/hr, that means 48 mph. If the speed limit is 100, (rare in Costa Rica), that means 60 mph.

WEBSITES

- www.visitcostarica.com The official site of the Costa Rica Tourist Board has lots of good general information. There's also a database of hotels and tour operators, which is quite extensive, but hard to get to: click on "Online Reservations" to find it.
- www.costaricaclick.com is a local web directory.
- www.cibercentro.com/costarica has links to local search engines, internet providers and other useful sites.
- www.ticotimes.net is the site of the English-language Tico Times.
- www.nacion.com is the site of the largest local newspaper.
- www.ecotourism.org is the site of the International Ecotourism Society, and includes lists of environmentally friendly lodges and tour operators.
- www.tripadvisor.com and www.virtualtourist.com have comments from fellow tourists about various attractions, lodgings and restaurants.

Privately-operated sites with varying amounts of useful information:

- www.costarica.com
- www.costaricabureau.com
- www.costa-rica-guide.com
- www.costarica-nationalparks.com
- www.costaricamap.com
- www.infocostarica.com

ESSENTIAL SPANISH

Pleasantries

Please - *por favor*
Thank you - *gracias*
You're welcome - *de nada*
Excuse me - *perdóneme* or *permiso*
Excuse me - *discúlpame*
Good day - *buenos días*
Good night - *buenas noches*
Goodbye - a*diós*
Hello - *hola*
How are you? - *¿How are you?*
Fine - *muy bien*
Pleased to meet you - *mucho gusto*

Everyday Phrases

Yes - *sí*
No - *no*
I don't know. - *No sé.*
Do you speak English? - *¿Habla usted inglés?*
I don't speak Spanish. - *Yo no hablo español.*
Where? - *¿Donde?*
When? - *¿Cuando?*
Why? - *¿Por que?*
How much? - *¿Cuanto?*
How do you say… - *¿Como se dice…?*
Today - *hoy*
Tomorrow - *mañana*
I would like - *quisiera*
Here - *aquí*
There - *allá*

More - *mas*
Less - *menos*
Much - *mucho*
Little - *poco*
Large - *grande*
Small - *pequeño*
Good - *bueno*
Bad - *malo*
What a deal! - *¡Que ganga!*

Travel Terms
Hotel - *(el) hotel*
Bank - *(el) banco*
Money - *(el) dinero*
Airport - *(el) aeropuerto*
Taxi - *(el) taxi*
Bus - *(el) autobús*
Car - *(el) coche, carro*
Bathrooms - *(los) baños*
Gas station - *(la) bomba, gasolinera*
How far is . . . - *¿Que distancia es . . . ?*
Road, highway - *(la) carretera*

Eating & Drinking (*comer y tomar*)
Meat - *(la) carne*
Beef - *(el) bistéc*
Pork - *(el) cerdo*
Chicken - *(el) pollo*
Fish - *(el) pescado*
Seafood - *(los) mariscos*
Shrimp - *(los) camarones*
Vegetables - *(los) legumbres*
Fruits - *(las) frutas*
Pineapple - *(la) piña*
Banana - *(el) plátano, banano*
Orange - *(la) naranja*
Apple - *(la) manzana*
Blackberry - *(la) mora*
Guava - *(la) guayaba*
Water - *(el) agua*

Milk - *(la) leche*
Coffee - *(el) café*
Tea - *(el) té*
Beer - *(la) cerveza*
Red Wine/White Wine - *vino tinto/vino blanco*
Glass (of water) - *(la) taza de agua*
Glass of wine - *(la) copa de vino*
Soft drink - *(el) refresco*
Smoothie - *(el) batido*
Juice - *(el) jugo*

Costa Rican Terms
Águila - slang name for Imperial beer, after the eagle on the label
Beneficio - coffee factory
Bomba - gas station
Buena nota - good, OK
Chapulines - youth gangs
Chepe - local name for San José
Chorizo - bribe (literally, a sausage)
Chunche - thing
¡Que chuso! - cool!
¿Cómo amaneció? - How did you wake up? Used for "good morning."
Fauna silvestre - wildlife
Ganja - marijuana (actually Jamaican slang)
Guaro - local cane liquor
Hora americana - more or less on time
Hora tica - mañana time
Mae, Maje - "dummy," used in a nice, kidding way like "pal"
María - taxi meter
Mota - marijuana
Pulpería - small grocery store
Precarista - squatter
¡Pura vida! - all-purpose interjection (literally, "pure life")
Sendero - nature trail
Soda - luncheonette or small restaurant
Tico(a) - Costa Rican person
¡Upe! - Is anyone home? (used instead of knocking)

Pronunciation

It's important to have a basic idea of pronunciation, so you can pronounce place names correctly. Spanish is a phonetic language, meaning that words are almost always spelled just as they sound.

Vowels are pronounced roughly as follows:
* a - as in *father*
* e - between *e* in *get* and *a* in *same*
* i - as in *magazine*
* o - as in *phone*
* u - as in *prune*

There are no silent vowels. For example, *coche* (car) is pronounced KO-chay.

A written accent on a vowel means that it is stressed, as in San José (pronounced sahn ho-SAY).

Consonants are pronounced roughly the same as in English, except:
* c - like *k* before *a, o* or *u*; like *s* before *e* or *i*
* h - always silent
* j - like *h* in *home*
* ll - like *y* in *yet*
* ñ - like *ni* in *union*
* z - like *s*

INDEX

Things Change!

Phone numbers, prices, addresses, quality of service – all change. If you come across any new information, we'd appreciate hearing from you. No item is too small! Drop us an e-mail at jopenroad@aol.com, visit us at www.openroadguides.com, or write us at:

Open Road's Best of Costa Rica
Open Road Publishing
P.O. Box 284
Cold Spring Harbor, NY 11724

TravelNotes

TravelNotes

TravelNotes

TravelNotes

TravelNotes

About the Author
Charlie Morris updated Open Road's previous Costa Rica and Belize guides for the past few editions, and is the author of our *Switzerland Guide*. When we decided to completely revamp our travel guides, we turned to Charlie and his vast Costa Rica expertise to write an all-new guide to this beautiful country. A former long-time resident of Costa Rica, Morris now lives in Treasure Island, Florida.

The New Open Road Travel Guides

Open Road has launched a radical new concept in travel guides: matching the time you *really* have for your vacation with the right amount of information you need for your perfect trip! No fluff, just the best things to do and see, the best places to stay and eat. Includes one-day, weekend, one-week and two-week trip ideas. It's the *perfect* travel guide!

Open Road's Best of Costa Rica, $14.95
Open Road's Best of Honduras, $14.95
Open Road's Best of Las Vegas, $14.95
Open Road's Best of Arizona, $14.95
Open Road's Best of Ireland, $14.95

And look for new guides to California, Italy, Belize, The Bahamas, The Caribbean and more in 2007!

Family Travel
Italy with Kids, $16.95
Paris with Kids, $16.95
Caribbean with Kids, $14.95
London with Kids, $14.95
New York City with Kids, $14.95
National Parks With Kids, $14.95
L.A. with Kids, $14.95
Washington, DC with Kids, $14.95
Hawaii with Kids, $14.95

Menu Translators
Eating & Drinking in Paris, $9.95
Eating & Drinking in Italy, $9.95
Eating & Drinking in Spain, $9.95

Made Easy Sights & Walks Guides
New York City Made Easy, $9.95
San Francisco Made Easy, $9.95
Amsterdam Made Easy, $9.95
Berlin Made Easy, $9.95
Dublin Made Easy, $9.95
Europe Made Easy, $10.95
Florence Made Easy, $9.95
Paris Made Easy, $9.95
Provence Made Easy, $9.95
Rome Made Easy, $9.95
Venice Made Easy, $9.95

**Order now at
www.openroadguides.com**